AL-FĀRĀBĪ'S SHORT COMMENTARY
ON ARISTOTLE'S *PRIOR ANALYTICS*

AL-FĀRĀBĪ'S SHORT COMMENTARY ON ARISTOTLE'S *PRIOR ANALYTICS*

*Translated from the Original Arabic
with Introduction and Notes*

BY

NICHOLAS RESCHER

Professor of Philosophy in the University of Pittsburgh

UNIVERSITY OF PITTSBURGH PRESS
1963

Library of Congress Catalog Card Number 63-10581

This book is dedicated,
with gratitude and with love,
to my mother
and
to the memory of my father.

PREFACE

This English version of al-Fārābī's "Short Commentary on *Prior Analytics*", made from Mlle Mubahat Türker's recent edition of the Arabic text (*Revue de la Faculté des Langues, d'Histoire, et de Géographie de l'Université d'Ankara*, vol. 16 [1958]), is the first appearance of this treatise in a European language. It is hoped that this addition to the dozen or so Arabic logical texts now accessible to the non-Orientalist will contribute to a wider appreciation of the great mass of work constituting the Arabic contribution to logic, which remains so largely *terra incognita*.

I wish to thank Mrs. Shukrieh Kassis and especially Mr. Seostoris Khalil for help with the translation. I am indebted to Mr. Storrs McCall, Dr. J. Ackrill, and particularly to Professor D. M. Dunlop for reading my typescript and suggesting needed improvements. Although some strengths of this work owe their existence to others, all of its weaknesses and errors must be laid at my own door.

I am grateful to Miss Dorothy Henle for performing the taxing task of preparing the typescript with her customary efficiency and accuracy.

This translation is part of a series of studies of Arabic contributions to logic supported by a grant from the National Science Foundation, which has facilitated both the accomplishment of the work, and its publication. It affords me great pleasure to record my sincere thanks for this assistance.

N. R.

PITTSBURGH
January 1963

TABLE OF CONTENTS

	PAGE
PREFACE	7
INTRODUCTION	11
1. Al-Fārābī	11
2. Al-Fārābī's Logical Work	12
3. Al-Fārābī's Logical Heritage	17
4. The Pursuit of "Aristotelian" Logic in the 8th and 9th Centuries, and the Subject of "Analytics"	20
5. Greek Commentaries on *Anal. Pr.*	23
6. Syriac Translations of and Commentaries on *Anal. Pr.*	27
7. Arabic Translations of and Commentaries on *Anal. Pr.* before Al-Fārābī	31
8. Al-Fārābī's Short Commentary on *Prior Analytics*	34
9. Analysis of Al-Fārābī's Short Commentary on *Anal. Pr.*	35
10. The Composition of Al-Fārābī's *Short Commentary* as Contrasted with *Anal. Pr.*	37
11. Items of Special Interest in Al-Fārābī's Short Commentary on *Anal. Pr.*	41
12. Some Points of Mechanics	44
AL-FĀRĀBĪ'S SHORT COMMENTARY ON ARISTOTLE'S *PRIOR ANALYTICS*	49
1. INTRODUCTION	49
2. CATEGORICAL PROPOSITIONS	52
3. CATEGORICAL SYLLOGISMS	60
4. CONDITIONAL SYLLOGISMS	74
5. "OBJECTING" SYLLOGISMS	81

		PAGE
6.	COMPOUND SYLLOGISMS	83
7.	INDUCTION	88
8.	INFERENCE BY "TRANSFER" (i.e., ANALOGY)	93
	1. The Method of "Transfer"	93
	2. The Method of "Investigation"	98
	3. Establishing Universal Premisses by the Methods of "Raising" and "Finding"	103
	4. The Types of "Transfer"	108
9.	THE "FOUR PRINCIPLES" FOR ESTABLISHING STATEMENTS	112
	1. Universal Substituted for Universal	113
	2. Universal Substituted for Particular	114
	3. Particular Substituted for Universal	116
	4. "Example" (i.e., Particular Substituted for Particular)	125
10.	CONCLUSION	131

INTRODUCTION

1. *Al-Fārābī*

Al-Fārābī, or, to give him his full name, Abū Naṣr Muḥammad ibn Muḥammad ibn Tarkhān ibn Uzalāj al-Fārābī, was born in Farab (Turkestan) not long after 870. Though his family was Muslim (of Turkish origin), he received his education in philosophy and the sciences under Christian (Nestorian) teachers, first in Khorasan, principally in Baghdad. His studies gave particular emphasis to logic, especially as a pupil of the important Nestorian logician and scholar Abū Bishr Mattā ibn Yūnus, who made the first Arabic translations of Aristotle's *Posterior Analytics* and *Poetics*.

Upon completing his studies, al-Fārābī lived the life of a scholar, principally at Baghdad and Aleppo. He was a teacher of philosophy of considerable importance. It is reported that he "read" (i.e., with a group of pupils) Aristotle's *Physics* forty times and his *Rhetoric* two hundred times.

Among the writings of al-Fārābī, his commentaries on Aristotle are of particular importance. They earned him the epithet of "the second teacher", i.e., the successor to Aristotle, the first teacher. His commentaries go beyond the works of Aristotle, however, to include various other Greek philosophical and scientific works, including the *Almagest* of Ptolemy. He also wrote original treatises on many subjects, his studies on music, political philosophy, and to a lesser extent the physical sciences, being of special interest and importance.

Having attained a considerable renown and influence, al-Fārābī died at great age, in 950, reportedly killed by robbers in the neighborhood of Damascus, while on a journey.

Al-Fārābī must be numbered with Ibn Sīnā (Avicenna), al-Ghazzālī, Ibn Rushd (Averroes), and Ibn Khaldūn among the very greatest philosophers of Islam.[1] Due largely to the enthusiastic recommendation of Maimonides, his writings played an important role in medieval Jewish thought. Moreover, some half-dozen of his works were translated into Latin in medieval times, and thus *Alfarabi* came to play a direct role in the work of the Christian scholastics, as well as an indirect role thanks to citations by other authors.

Al-Fārābī devoted more effort to logic than to any other single branch of philosophy or science. He deserves to be classified as the first specialist in logical studies among the Arabic-speaking peoples, with the possible exception of his teacher, Abū Bishr Mattā ibn Yūnus, who, however, was rooted in the Syriac milieu and was primarily rather a translator of logical texts than a student of logic.

2. *Al-Fārābī's Logical Work*

Al-Fārābī wrote commentaries on the entire Aristotelian logical Organon (including the *Rhetorica* and *Poetica*), treating much of it in the triplicate manner typical of the Arabic commentators (Epitome = Short Commentary, Middle Commentary, and Great Commentary), following in Alexandrian footsteps. He also produced various short studies devoted to special points. The bibliographical survey of al-Fārābī's writings by Ahmet Ateş[2] lists over forty treatises on logical matters, of which at best some twenty appear to have survived. The following have been published:

---

[1] Only two book-length studies of the philosophy of al-Fārābī exist to date, Moritz Steinschneider's century-old classic, *Al-Farabi: Des Arabischen Philosophen Leben und Schriften* (Mémoires de l'Académie Impériale des Sciences de Saint-Pétersbourg; VIIe série, vol. 13, no. 4; St. Pétersbourg, 1869); and Ibrahim Madkour, *La Place d'al-Fārābī dans l'École Philosophique Musulmane* (Paris, 1934). For a comprehensive inventory of printed discussions related to al-Fārābī, see N. Rescher, *Al-Fārābī: An Annotated Bibliography* (Pittsburgh, 1962).

[2] Ahmet Ateş, "Fārābī bibliografyasi", *Türk Tarih Kurumu Belleten* (Ankara), vol. 15 (1951), pp. 175–192. A bibliography listing all identifiable works of al-Fārābī and giving data on manuscript locations and editions, where possible.

Kitāb al-tautiʾah fī-'l-manṭiq ("Preparation for Logic") or *Kitāb al-madkhal ilā-'l-manṭiq* ("Introduction to Logic").
1. (Edition) D. M. Dunlop. "Al-Fārābī's *Eisagoge*." *The Islamic Quarterly*, vol. 3 (1956), pp. 117–138.
2. (Edition) Mubahat Türker. "Fārābī'nin bazi mantik eserleri." ("Some Logical Works of Farabi" in Turkish). *Revue de la Faculté de Langues, d'Histoire et de Géographie de l'Université d'Ankara*; vol. 16 (1958), pp. 165–286.
3. (Translation—English) D. M. Dunlop. See 1 above.
4. (Translation—Turkish) Mubahat Türker. See 2 above.

Risālah ṣudirah bi-hā al-kitāb ("Treatise With Which the Book (=??) Begins").
1. (Edition) D. M. Dunlop. "Al-Fārābī's Introductory *Risālah* on Logic." *The Islamic Quarterly*, vol. 3 (1956–1957), pp. 224–235.
2. (Translation—English) D. M. Dunlop. See 1 above.

Sharḥ kitāb al-maqūlāt li-Arisṭūṭālīs (*ʿalā jiḥah al-taʿālīq*) ("Commentary on Aristotle's *Categoriae* [in the Form of Remarks]").
1. (Edition) D. M. Dunlop. "Al-Fārābī's Paraphrase of the *Categories* of Aristotle." *The Islamic Quarterly*, vol. 4 (1958), pp. 168–197; vol. 5 (1959), pp. 21–54.
2. (Edition) Nihat Keklik. "Abū Naṣr al-Fārābī'nin Katagoriler Kitabi." *Review of the Institute of Islamic Studies* (Publications of the Faculty of Letters, Istanbul University); vol. 2 (1960), parts 2–4; pp. 48.
3. (Translation—English) D. M. Dunlop. See 1 above.

Sharḥ kitāb al-ʿibārah li-Arisṭūṭālīs ("[Great] Commentary on Aristotle's *De Interpretatione*").
1. (Edition) W. Kutsch and S. Marrow. *Al-Fārābī's Commentary on Aristotle's Peri Hermēneias (De Interpretatione)*. Beirut, 1961.

Kitāb al-qiyās al-ṣaghīr ("Short Book [i.e., Short Commentary] on the Syllogism [i.e., on *Prior Analytics*, the 'Book of the Syllogism']").

1. (Edition) Mubahat Türker. "Fārābī'nin bazi mantik eserleri." ("Some Logical Works of Fārābī" in Turkish). *Revue de la Faculté de Langues, d'Histoire et de Géographie de l'Université d'Ankara*; vol. 16 (1958), pp. 165–286.
2. (Translation—Turkish) Mubahat Türker. See 1 above.
3. (Translation—English) Nicholas Rescher. The present work.

Risālah fī jawāb masā'il su'ilā ʿan-hā ("Answers to Questions Put to Him").

1. (Edition) Friederich Dieterici. *Alfārābī's Philosophische Abhandlungen*. Leiden, 1890.
2. (Edition) Abd-al-Raḥīm Makkawī. *Majmūʿ falsafah Abī Naṣr al-Fārābī*. Cairo (Saʿādah Press), 1325 A.H. (1907). P. 176. Reprinted Cairo, 1926.
3. (Edition) Anonymous (editor). *Al-Fārābī: Risālah fī masā'il mutafarriqah*. Hyderabad (Dā'irah al-Maʿarif), 1344 A.H. (1925), p. 26.
4. (Edition) Anonymous (editor). *Rasā'il al-Fārābī*. Hyderabad (Dā'irah al-Maʿārif), 1350 A.H. (1931).
5. (Edition) Anonymous (editor). *Rasā'il al-Fārābī*. Bombay, 1354 A.H. (1937).
6. (Translation—German) Friederich Dieterici. *Alfārābī's Philosophische Abhandlungen*. Leiden, 1892.
7. (Translation—Turkish; partial) Kivameddin Burslan. *Uzluk oğlu Farabi'nin eserlerinden seçme paraçalar*. Istanbul (Devlet Matbassi), 1935. P. 87.
8. (Translation—Turkish) Kivameddin Burslan and Hilmi Ziya Ülken. *Fārābī* (in Turkish). Istanbul, 1941.
9. (Study) Nicholas Rescher. "A Ninth-Century Arabic Logician on: Is Existence a Predicate?" *Journal of the History of Ideas*, vol. 21 (1960), pp. 428–430.

Kitāb sharā'iṭ al-burhān ("Book on the Conditions of Demonstration"). Extract—*Fuṣūl yuḥtāj ilai-hā fī ṣinā'ah al-manṭiq* ("Chapters Containing what is Needful for the Art of Logic").

1. (Edition; the extract) D. M. Dunlop. "Al-Fārābī's Introductory Sections on Logic." *The Islamic Quarterly*, vol. 2 (1955), pp. 264-282.
2. (Edition; the extract) Mubahat Türker. "Fārābī'nin bazi mantik eserleri." ("Some Logical Works of Farabi" in Turkish). *Revue de la Faculté de Langues, d'Histoire et de Géographie de l'Université of Ankara*; vol. 16 (1958), pp. 165-286.
3. (Translation—Medieval Latin excerpts) Dominique H. Salman. "Fragments inédits de la logique d'Alfarabi." *Revue des sciences philosophiques et théologiques*, vol. 32 (1948), pp. 222-225.
4. (Translation—French two extracts) Khalil Georr. "Bibliographie Critique de Fārābī, suivie de Deux Textes Inédits sur la Logique, accompagnés d'une traduction française et de notes." Unpublished doctoral dissertation submitted to the Faculté des Lettres of the Université de Paris, May 1945. P. 265.
5. (Translation of the extract—English) D. M. Dunlop. See 1 above.
6. (Translation of the extract—Turkish) Mubahat Türker. See 2 above.
7. (Study, the extract only) Harry Blumberg. "Alfarabi's Five Chapters on Logic." *Proceedings of the American Academy for Jewish Research*, vol. 6 (1934-1935), pp. 115-121.
8. (Study) Nicholas Rescher. "On the Provenance of the *Logica Alpharabii*." *The New Scholasticism*, vol. 37 (1963).

Liber introductorius in artem logicae demonstrationis. [Attributed to F, but actually this epitome of *Anal. Post.* is a

part of the Encyclopedia of the "Brethren of Purity" (*Ikhwān al-Ṣafā'*).]
1. (Edition) Friederich Dieterici. *Die Abhandlungen der Ichwān es-Safā* (in Auswahl arabisch herausgegeben von F. D.). Two vols., Leipzig, 1883, 1886.
2. (Translation—German) Friederich Dieterici. *Die Logik und Psychologie der Araber im Zehnten Jahrhundert.* Leipzig, 1868.
3. (Translation—Latin and German) Albino Nagy. *Die Philosophischen Abhandlungen des ... al-Kindī.* (*Beiträge zur Geschichte der Philosophie des Mittelalters.* II 5 (1897)). Pp. xxiv, 84.
4. (Study) Henry George Farmer. "Who was the Author of the '*Liber introductorius in artem logicae demonstrationis*'?" *Journal of the Royal Asiatic Society,* 1934, pp. 553–556.
5. (Study) Henry George Farmer. *Al-Fārābī's Arabic-Latin Writings on Music: The Texts, Edited with Translations and Commentaries.* Glasgow, 1934.
6. (Authorship) Franz Rosenthal. *Aḥmad b. aṭ-Ṭayyib as-Sarakhsī* (New Haven, 1943), p. 57.

Sharḥ kitāb al-khaṭābah li-Arisṭū (*Declaratio compendiosa super libris rhetoricorum Aristotelis*).
1. (Translation—Medieval Latin) *Alfarabius: Declaratio compendiosa super libris rhetoricorum Aristotillis* (sic). Venice, 1484.
2. (Translation—Medieval Latin) *Rhetorica Aristotelis— nec non Alpharabii compendiosa declaratione*: edidit Alexander Achillinus. Venice, 1515.
3. (Translation — Medieval Latin — introduction only) Amable Jourdain. *Recherches critiques sur l'âge et l'origine des traductions latines d'Aristote.* Paris, 1843. (Nouvelle édition par Charles Jourdain.) Pp. xv, 472. Photoreprinted, N.Y., 1960.
4. (Study) Albino Nagy. "Notizie intorno alla retorica d'Al-Fārābī." *Rendiconti della Reale Accademia dei*

Lincei (Classe di Scienze Morali, Storiche, e Filologiche), Serie 5, vol. II; Rome 1893; pp. 684-691.

Ṣadr kitāb al-khaṭābah (*Declaratio compendiosa per viam divisionis super libris rhetoricorum Aristotelis*).
1. (Translation—Medieval Latin) *Declaratio compendiosa per viam divisionis Alpharabii super libris rhetoricorum Aristotilis.* Venetiis, 1481.
2. (Study) Albino Nagy. "Notizie intorno alla retorica d'Al-Fārābī." *Rendiconti della Reale Accademia dei Lincei* (Classe di Scienze Morali, Storiche, e Filologiche), Serie 5, vol. II; Rome 1893, pp. 684-691.

Risālāh fī qawānīn ṣināʿah al-shiʿr ("Treatise on the Canons of the Art of Poetry").
1. (Edition) A. J. Arberry. "Fārābī's Canons of Poetry." *Rivista degli Studi Orientali*, vol. 17 (1938), pp. 266-278.
2. (Edition) Abderrahman Badawī. *Aristoteles: De Poetica e graeco transtulit, commentis auxit ac critica editione antiquae Arabicae versiones et Alfarabi, Avicennae Averroisque commentariorum.* Le Caire, 1953. Pp. 261, 53.
3. (Translation—English) A. J. Arberry. See 1 above.

Kitāb fīʾl-shiʿr wa-ʾl-qawāfī ("Book on Poetry and Metrics") or *Kitāb al-shiʿr* ("Book on Poetry").
1. (Edition) Muḥsin Mahdī. "Kitāb al-shiʿr li-Abī Naṣr al-Fārābī." *Shiʿr* (periodical published in Beirut, Lebanon), vol. 3 (no. 12; 1959), pp. 91-96.

3. *Al-Fārābī's Logical Heritage*

Thanks to the great medical history of Ibn Abī Uṣaibiʿah[1]

---

[1] *ʿUyūn al-anbāʾ fī ṭabaqāt al-aṭibbāʾ* ("The Sources of Information about the Classes of Physicians"), edited by August Müller (as "Die Reihen der Ärtzte"), vol. 1, Cairo, 1882 (text only), vol. 2, Königsberg, 1884 (notes). The extract in question occurs in vol. I, from page 134, line 30 to page 135, line 24.

we are able to read, in an extensive quotation from an otherwise lost work of al-Fārābī's "On the Appearance of Philosophy", as follows:

> Then [i.e., after the rise of Islam] the instruction [in logic] was moved from Alexandria to Antioch and remained there for a long time until at last but one teacher remained. With him there studied two men, and they moved away taking the books with them. Now one of them was of the people of Ḥarrān, and the other of the people of Marw. As to the one of the people of Marw, there studied with him two men, one of whom was Ibrāhīm al-Marwazī and the other Yūḥannā ibn Ḥailān. With al-Marwazī studied the bishop Isrāʿīl and Quwairī, both of whom went to Baghdad. Now Ibrāhīm [sic. in error for Isrāʿīl] occupied himself with his [i.e., Christian] religion. Ibrāhīm al-Marwazī went down to Baghdad and settled there. With al-Marwazī studied Mattā ibn Yūnān [i.e., Abū Bishr Mattā ibn Yūnus].
>
> That which was taught [in logic] at that time was up to the end of the assertoric figures [of the syllogism]. But Abū Naṣr al-Fārābī says about himself that he studied with Yūḥannā ibn Ḥailān up to the end of *Anal. Post.* (*kitāb al-burhān*). The part [of the two *Analytics*] which comes after the assertoric figures (of the syllogism [i.e., which comes after *Anal. Pr.*, I, 7]) was called "the part which is not read" until [the time when] one read that; for it became standard [in logical study] afterwards. When the matter came to Muslim teachers one read from the assertoric figures as far as a man was able to read. And thus Abū Naṣr [al-Fārābī] says that he himself read [i.e., under a teacher] up to the end of *Anal. Post.*

We are in a position to supplement al-Fārābī's data about his teachers from other sources,[2] with the following result regarding the "genealogy" of master-and-pupil kinship:

[2] For the most part, the data have been compiled and analyzed in the magisterial study of Max Meyerhof, "Von Alexandrien nach Baghdad: Ein Beitrag zur Geschichte des philosophischen und medizinischen Unterrichts bei den Arabern", *Sitzungsberichte der Preussischen Akademie der Wissenschaften, Philosophisch-historische Klasse*, vol. 23, Berlin, 1930, pp. 389–429. For our text see pp. 393–394 and 404–405. And see also Meyerhof's paper on "La Fin de

Introduction 19

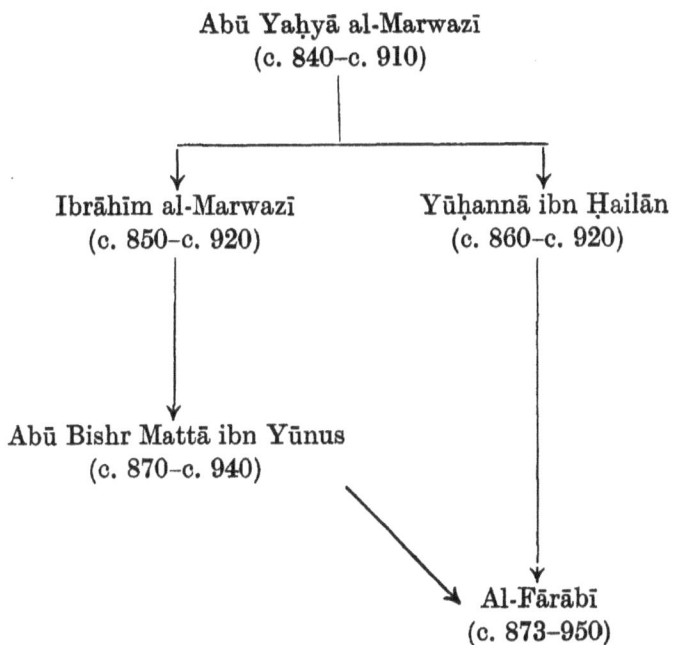

All of al-Fārābī's teachers are identifiable personages about whose life and work we possess considerable information. But not only does al-Fārābī's account shed interesting light upon the study of Aristotle's logic among the Christian scholars, primarily Nestorians, who carried Greek logic from Alexandria to Baghdad in the 9th century,[3] it furnishes an important datum about al-Fārābī himself. It shows that this first of Arabic logicians must be regarded as a continuator of the logical work of the Syrian Christian logicians, and perhaps to some extent even as simply a transmitter into Arabic of the scholarship of his Syrian predecessors. Rather than impugning al-Fārābī's originality, this lack of

---

l'École d'Alexandrie d'après quelques Auteurs Arabes", *Bulletin de l'Institut d'Égypte*, vol. 15 (1932–1933), pp. 109–123 (especially pp. 114–118).
[3] For further information along these lines, see N. Rescher, "Al-Fārābī on Logical Tradition", *The Journal of the History of Ideas*, vol. 24 (1963), pp. 127–132.

strict independence is precisely what establishes his claims to the heritage of Greek learning, and his status as a "second teacher" of Aristotelian logic.

4. *The Pursuit of "Aristotelian" Logic in the 8th and 9th Centuries, and the Subject of "Analytics"*

The Syriac-speaking Christian sects cultivated the Greek mathematical, astronomical, and medical writers, as well as the Greek philosophers. All of these branches of learning were pursued in close conjunction with theological studies, for Greek science and philosophy provided the intellectual rationale within which the theology of these churches found its articulation. Medicine especially formed a bridge between the sciences and theology, and many of the Syriac Christian theologians were trained as physicians of the body as well as the soul. And as we shall see, logic was at this juncture an integral part of curriculum of medical studies, as in Alexandria (mem. Galen).

The Syrian Christian academies divided their curriculum into two parts: an elementary program preparatory for more advanced work in one or more of three areas of speciality: astronomy, medicine, and theology. For example the Nestorian academy at Jundi-Shapur (between Baghdad and Isfahan) had also a medical faculty (with an attached hospital) and a faculty of astronomy (with an observatory). Along with mathematics, logic was a central subject of the preparatory program, and thus played an important part as a common bridge between the various branches of learning. This organization of the educational curriculum is reflected in the ordering of the sciences by the Syriac-speaking philosophers: logic, mathematics, physics (including psychology), and theology. It is thus not surprising to find many cases similar to that of the distinguished Monophysite theologian Severus Sebhokht (d. 666/7) who wrote important treatises on logic and astronomy as well as theology. These arrangements follow Alexandrian precedent, and the Syriac tradition was throughout continuous with that of Hellenistic Alexandria.

A good deal of information as to the Syriac translations of Aristotle's logic is available; indeed much of this work has survived, and some of it has been published. Porphyry's *Isagoge* was put at the head of the logical Organon as an introduction. The *Rhetorica* and *Poetica* were added at the end (although Syriac writers—like their Arabic successors— were troubled by the latter work, since Greek literature, in contrast to Greek science and philosophy, was virtually a closed book to them).

As a result, the Syriac expositors of Aristotelian logic arrived at the following standard arrangement of logical works: *Isagoge* (Porphyry), *Categoriae*, *De Interpretatione*, *Analytica Priora*, *Analytica Posteriora*, *Topica*, *Sophistici Elenchi*, *Rhetorica*, and *Poetica*. These nine works were thought of as dealing with nine respective *distinct branches* of logic, each based upon its canonical text. This construction of Aristotelian logic was taken over by the Arabs, resulting in the following organization of the subject matter of logic:

Branch	Arabic Name[1]	Basic Text
(1) "Introduction"	al-īsāghūjī	*Isagoge* (Porphyry)
(2) Categories	al-maqūlāt	*Categoriae*
(3) Hermeneutics	al-'ibārah	*De Interpretatione*
(4) Analytics	al-qiyās	*Analytica Priora*
(5) Apodictics	al-burhān	*Analytica Posteriora*
(6) Topics	al-jadal	*Topica*
(7) Sophistics	al-mughāliṭah (or al-safsaṭah)	*Sophistici Elenchi*
(8) Rhetoric	al-khiṭābah	*Rhetorica*
(9) Poetics	al-shi'r	*Poetica*

The totality of this Organon was referred to as "the nine

[1] There is, however, considerable variation in this nomenclature, especially in the earlier times. For information on this subject, see the *Kitāb al-Fihrist* of Ibn al-Nadīm.

books" of logic, or as "the eight books" with the *Poetica* (or sometimes *Isagoge*) excluded. The first four of these logical treatises (which apparently were the only ones translated into Syriac prior to A.D. 800) were called "the four books" of logic. It was these "four books" which constituted the object of logical studies in the basic curriculum of the Syriac academies. It was not by accident that in the study of Aristotle's logic among the Syriac Christians "the four books" were emphasized and taken as the basis for logical studies. *Anal. Post.* was, as we have seen, viewed as suspect for theological reasons, and the emphasis thus fell on its predecessors. This did not mean that scholars did not read the other logical treatises, but they remained the province of experts, whereas ordinary students limited themselves to "the four books".

The instructional role of the Aristotelian treatises led to a triplication of the commentaries upon them. There were *Short Commentaries* or *Epitomes*, *Middle Commentaries*, and *Great* or *Long Commentaries*. Each of these has a distinctive format. A Great Commentary first *quotes* verbatim a section of the Aristotelian text a few sentences in length, and then gives a detailed discussion of this quotation, generally two or three times its length, which frequently takes the views of the Greek commentators into account. A Middle Commentary *paraphrases* Aristotle and offers supplemental explanatory discussions. It is usually somewhat longer than its original. An Epitome *presents the gist* of an Aristotelian work and may also offer introductory remarks about the subject-matter, or about the place of the work in the Aristotelian corpus. It is generally about half the length of its subject work. This threefold arrangement of the logical commentaries corresponds to the program of instruction in the Syrian academies: the Epitome for the first cycle of study, the Middle Commentary for the second, the Great Commentary for the third. Education did not proceed by continuous acquisition of new materials, but by iterative deepening of material already familiar.

Introduction

In time, each "branch" of logic acquired, under the impact of the tradition of instruction, certain distinctive features which involved departures from the materials of the basic text. We shall see, for example, how al-Fārābī's treatment of "analytics" involves both deletions from and additions to the subject-materials of *Anal. Pr.*

Virtually all of these details regarding the character of Aristotelian logic in its Syriac guise were passed on to the Arabs. This includes such matters as the organization of the logical works, the emphasis upon the "four books", the place of logic among the sciences, the role of logic in the program of instruction in medicine and astronomy (but not, in Islam, in theological instruction—at any rate prior to the scholasticization of the *madrasahs* which began in the late 13th century).

The first generations of Arabic writers on philosophy and logic, including such men as al-Kindī, al-Rāzī, and al-Fārābī, were in a real sense the "products" of the Syriac schools, in that they acquired their knowledge from men trained in them. This Syriac tradition transmitted to the Arabs not only the matter of Greek scholarship, but its forms as well. The Arabic logicians are thus the continuators of the work of the Hellenistic Greeks, and Muslim Aristotelians such as al-Fārābī and Averroes are later links in a chain whose earlier members include such Greek-language scholars as Alexander of Aphrodisias, Porphyry, Themistius, Ammonius, and Philoponus.[2]

5. *Greek Commentaries on* Anal. Pr.

Unquestionably there are many ancient Greek studies of or commentaries upon *Prior Analytics* of which all traces

[2] This discussion of the character of logical studies in the Syriac-speaking orbit is drawn primarily from the following works: Anton Baumstark, *Aristoteles bei den Syrern* (Leipzig, 1900); Khalil Georr, *Les Catégories d'Aristote dans leurs Versions Syro-Arabes* (Beyrouth, 1948); Max Meyerhof, "Von Alexandrien Nach Baghdad" (see above); De Lacy O'Leary, *How Greek Science Passed to the Arabs* (London, 1949).

have been lost. However, the identifiable ones which postdate the great Megarian and Stoic logicians are as follows:[1]

(A) *Galen* (129–c. 199), the famous physician, wrote extensively on philosophy in general and logic in particular. Among his numerous treatises on logic, several deal with the materials of *Anal. Pr.*[2] The only one of these works known to have survived is an *Introduction to Logic* (*Eisagōgē dialectikē*), first published by Minoides Minas in 1844.[3]

(B) *Herminus* (c. 130–c. 190), the teacher of Alexander of Aphrodisias, wrote:

(1) A commentary on *Anal. Pr.*

This work, reportedly taking a highly independent position, disagreeing with Aristotle on important points, has unhappily not survived.

(C) *Alexander of Aphrodisias* (c. 160–c. 220), who was active at Athens, where he held the chair in peripatetic philosophy from 198 to 211, was a most diligent student of Aristotle, and wrote, among many other commentaries,

(2) A commentary on Book I of *Anal. Pr.*

This survives, and was published several times during the Renaissance, as was a Latin translation by

---

[1] The ensuing catalogue is based in the main on Karl Praechter's volume on *Die Philosophie des Altertums* (Berlin, 1926) in the revised series of Friederich Ueberweg's *Grundriss der Geschichte der Philosophie*.

[2] These are listed in chapters 12 and 15–16 of Galen's treatise *Peri tōn idiōn bibliōn* (*De libris propriis*), see pp. 43–47 of volume 19 of C. G. Kühn's edition of Galen's *Opera Omnia* (Leipzig, 1830).

[3] Edited by Carl Kalbfleisch, *Galeni Institutio Logica* (Leipzig, 1896). Idem, "Über Galen's Einleitung in die Logik", *Jahrbuch für klassische Philologie*, Supplement 23 (1897), pp. 679–708. Ivan Müller, "Galen's Werk vom wissenschaftlichen Beweis", *Abhandlungen der K. Akad. der Wissenschaften in München* (Philos.-philol. Klasse), vol. 20, pt. 2 (1895), pp. 403 ff. J. Mau, *Galen: Einführung in die Logik* (Berlin, 1960).

Feliciano (Venice, 1542). The Greek text was edited in 1883 by Maximilian Wallies in the Berlin Academy *Commentaria in Aristotelem Graeca* series (vol. 2, pt. 1).[4] Alexander also wrote a (lost) treatise on modally "mixed" syllogisms.

(D) *Porphyry* (232/3–c. 300), the famous philosopher and disciple of Plotinus, and author of the *Isagoge*, wrote a treatise on categorical syllogisms, and commented on several parts of the Organon, certainly *Categoriae* and *De Interp.*, and very likely also *Anal. Pr.*[5]

(E) *Themistius* (317–c. 390), an influential teacher of philosophy at Constantinople, wrote:

(3) A paraphrase ("Short Commentary") on Book I of *Anal. Pr.*

This may survive in the version edited in 1884 by M. Wallies in the Berlin *Commentaria in Aristotelem Graeca* series (vol. 23, pt. 3).[6]

(F) *Ammonius* (c. 450–c. 520) was an important professor of philosophy at Alexandria, where John Philoponus, Simplicius, and Olympiodorus were among his pupils. He wrote:

---

[4] Regarding Alexander on *Anal. Pr.* see: G. Volait, *Die Stellung des Alexander von Aphrodisias zur aristotelischen Schlusslehre* (Halle, 1907); Bonn University *Inauguraldissertation*, also published in full in *Abhandlungen zur Philosophie und ihrer Geschichte*, Heft 27, and E. Thouverez, "Ein Bericht des Alexander von Aphrodisias über die peripatetische Syllogistik", *Archiv für Geschichte der Philosophie*, vol. 15 (1902), pp. 58 ff.

[5] See the list of Porphyry's works given in J. Bidez, *Vie de Porphyre* (Gand and Leipzig, 1913).

[6] Regarding Themistius' contributions to logic, see Valentin Rose, "Über eine angebliche Paraphrase des Themistius", *Hermes*, vol. 2 (1867), pp. 191–213. W. D. Ross, however, disagrees that the extant paraphrase attributed to Themistius is actually by him; believing that it may be due to Sophonias (fl. c. 1300). See his edition of *Aristotle's Prior and Posterior Analytics* (Oxford, 1957), p. 2.

(4) A commentary on Book I of *Anal. Pr.*

This survives, and was published during the Renaissance, as also was a Latin translation. The Greek text was edited in 1899 by M. Wallies in the Berlin *Commentaria in Aristotelem Graeca* (vol. 4, pt. 6).

(G) *John Philoponus* (c. 480–c. 540). After studying at Alexandria as a student of Ammonius, Philoponus settled there as a teacher (he may have succeeded Ammonius in the chair of philosophy). Late in his career, he converted to Christianity. He wrote:

(5) A commentary on *Anal. Pr.* (covering Book II as well as Book I, though much more briefly).

This survives and was edited in 1905 by M. Wallies in the Berlin *Commentaria in Aristotelem Graeca* (vol. 13, pt. 2).

(H) *Simplicius* (c. 490–c. 550), a pupil of Ammonius, was among the professors of philosophy at Athens who emigrated to Persia, to seek the protection of Chosroes Anushirwan, after Justinian closed the school of philosophy in Athens in 529. (He returned to Greece after some two years.) Although it seems certain that Simplicius lectured on *Anal. Pr.*, no such commentary has survived.

(I) *Olympiodorus* (c. 490–c. 560), a contemporary of Simplicius, and also a student of Ammonius, settled at Alexandria and was a successor (at one or two removes) of Ammonius in the chair of philosophy. He lectured on the Organon, but his comments on *Anal. Pr.* have not survived.

(J) *Elias* (c. 520–c. 580), the successor of Olympiodorus in the Alexandrian philosophy professoreate, wrote:

(6) Scholia on Book I of *Anal. Pr.*

These have survived and have been edited by L. E.

Introduction 27

Westernick, "Elias on the Prior Analytics", *Memnosyne*, vol. 14 (1961), pp. 134–139.

Although all six of the works listed above are available in print in modern scholarly editions of the highest standard, thanks primarily to the monumental and essentially single-handed efforts of Maximilian Wallies, they have been insufficiently studied, and stand in need of annotated modern-language translations, equipped with suitable informative and interpretative commentaries, to make them accessible to a wider range of interested students.

For our purposes, however, the most significant fact is that from the time of Ammonius (fl. c. 500) to that of Elias (fl. c. 570) and beyond there was in Alexandria *a continuous tradition of study of Aristotle's logic in general and of* Anal. Pr. *in particular*. This scholarly effort made use of older commentaries, particularly that of Alexander of Aphrodisias, and itself produced such substantial works as the commentaries of Ammonius and of John Philoponus. The *scholars* at the forefront of logical study among the Syriac-speaking peoples were in personal contact with, and in the literal sense the students of, these Alexandrian exponents of Aristotle's logic.[7]

6. *Syriac Translations of and Commentaries on* Anal. Pr.

The scholars of the Syriac-speaking Christian communities (Nestorians and Monophysites) of the eastern Mediterranean actively took up the study and propagation of Greek learning, beginning in the 4th century A.D. The Syriac contributions to the study of *Prior Analytics*, aside from general surveys of Aristotelian logic in which *Anal. Pr.* plays a subordinate part, may (so far as we know) be summarized

[7] The fullest account of the links between these two traditions is Max Meyerhof's monograph "Von Alexandrien nach Baghdad" (*Sitzungsberichte der Preussischen Akademie der Wissenschaften* (philosophisch-historische Klasse), vol. 23, 1930).

in the following tabulation.[1] This meager list certainly represents but a fraction of the work actually done.

(A) *Probha* (fl. c. 480), a Nestorian scholar, produced:

    (1) A short commentary on *Anal. Pr.*

This was edited, and translated into French, by A. van Hoonacker: "Le Traité du Philosophe Syrien Probus sur les Premiers Analytiques d'Aristote", *Journal Asiatique*, vol. 16 (1900), pp. 70–166. It is possible that Probha also made a Syriac translation of *Anal. Pr.* to I, 7.

(B) *Sergeius of Reshaina* (fl. c. 530), an eminent Monophysite physician, studied medicine and philosophy at Alexandria. He wrote:

    (2) A treatise on the relation of *Anal. Pr.* to Aristotle's other logical works.

    (3) A treatise on the concept of *schēma* in *Anal. Pr.*

Both of these works are extant, but have not yet been edited or studied.

(C) *Paulus Persa* (fl. c. 570) wrote:

    (4) A treatise (dedicated to the Persian monarch Chosroes Anushirwan) on the whole of Aristotelian logic, including *Anal. Pr.*

This treatise survived and has been edited by M. Land, in his *Anecdota Syrica*, with Latin translation and notes.

(D) *Severus Sebhokht* (fl. c. 630, d. 666/7), a Monophysite bishop, wrote:

    (5) A treatise on the (non-modal) syllogisms of *Anal. Pr.*

This treatise is also extant but unexplored.

---

[1] The ensuing account relies primarily upon Anton Baumstark, *Geschichte der Syrischen Literatur* (Bonn, 1922). I have also consulted

Introduction 29

(E) *Silvanus of Qardu* (fl. c. 640), a Nestorian scholar, wrote:

    (6) A short commentary (epitome) of *Anal. Pr.* as part of a series dealing with "the four books".

This has apparently not survived.

(F) *Athanasius of Baladh* (fl. c. 660, d. 686), a pupil of (D) above, and a patriarch in the Monophysite church, wrote:

    (7) An epitome of *Anal. Pr.* as part of a treatment of "the four books".

The whole treatise has been edited by Giuseppe Furlani, "Una Introduzione alla Logica Aristotelica di Atanasio di Balad", *Rendiconti della Reale Accademia dei Lincei* (Classe di Scienze Morali, Storiche e Filologiche), Serie 5, vol. 25 (Rome, 1916), pp. 717–778. [Syriac text edition (pp. 719–778).] A revised translation was published by Furlani in 1925: "L'introduzione di Atanasio de Bālādh alla logica e syllogistica aristotelica", *Atti del Reale Instituto Veneto di Scienze, Lettere, el Arti*, vol. 85 (1925–1926), part 2, pp. 319–344.

(G) *Henanishu I* (fl. c. 680, d. 699/700), a Nestorian patriarch, wrote:

    (9) A commentary on *Anal. Pr.*

This work has not survived.

(H) *Jacob of Edessa* (b. c. 640, d. 708), an eminent Jacobite scholar, and a pupil of (D) above, also studied in Alexandria, and made:

    (8) A Syriac translation of the "standard" part of *Anal. Pr.*, i.e., to I, 7.

This has apparently not survived.

Isidor Friedmann, *Aristotles Analytica bei den Syrern* (Berlin, 1898; Erlangen dissertation for 1898) and Rubens Duval, *La Littérature Syriaque* (Paris, 1899).

(I) *George, Bishop (Jacobite) of the Arabs* (fl. c. 690, d. 724, very old), a pupil of (G), made:
  (10) A Syriac translation of the *whole* (!) of *Anal. Pr.*, accompanied by,
  (11) A commentary on the *whole* (!) of this work.

George's translation is the best Syriac version of *Anal. Pr.* to that time. It and the conjoint commentary are multiply extant and have been published (Syriac text only; no translation) by Giuseppe Furlani: "Il Primo Libro dei Primi Analitici di Aristotele nella versione siriaca di Giorgio delle Nazioni", *Memorie della Reale Accademia Nazionale dei Lincei* (Classe di Scienzi Morali, Storiche e Filologiche), Serie 6, part 5, fasc. 3, vol. 332 (Roma, 1935); and "Il Secondo Libro . . .", *ibid.*, serie 6, part 6, fasc. 3, vol. 334 (Roma, 1937), pp. 233–286.

In general these Syriac translations and commentaries were made for students in the academies who had, among other preliminaries to medical and/or theological specialization, to master "the four books" of Aristotelian logic. The students apparently knew some Greek: technical terms are generally transliterated rather than translated. (See Furlani's Italian version of item (7).) Not until reasonably late (i.e., c. 670) is it felt necessary to retranslate the school-text portion *Anal. Pr.* into Syriac (item (8)) to improve upon a crude older version (of Probha?), and even then the practice was apparently to transliterate rather than translate the technical terms. A "smooth" version of *Anal. Pr.* is not provided until 690/700 (item (10)). Although the Syriac *scholars* maintained a continuous link with Greek-speaking Alexandria, their *students* seem gradually to have lost their Greek.

Throughout this Syriac work with the subject materials of *Anal. Pr.* there is no question of any original contributions to logic as a science, any more than there would be in (say) school studies of Euclid. Everything is a matter of accurate transmission of fixed knowledge in essentially stylized form. Such changes as come about are almost glacial in character, and relate to matters of emphasis rather than substance.

It should be stressed, however, that the Syriac logicians, even if unoriginal, kept alive at a reasonably sophisticated level the knowledge of Aristotelian logic, and maintained a living link, as visitors and as actual pupils, with the Aristotelians of Alexandria.

7. *Arabic Translations of and Commentaries on* Anal. Pr. *before Al-Fārābī*

The Syriac logicians, and the first generation of Arabic logicians who followed in their footsteps, sometimes wrote general accounts of the Aristotelian Organon, or of its first half (through *Anal. Pr.*). Apart from such general surveys, the Arabic work on *Anal. Pr.* prior to al-Fārābī, of which we now have knowledge, is as follows:[1]

(A) *Yaḥya (Yuḥannā) ibn al-Biṭrīq* (c. 770–c. 830) was a Christian scholar who probably converted to Islam. He specialized in Arabic translations of Greek scientific and philosophical texts, one of his most important translations being that of Plato's *Timaeus*. He made:

(1) An Arabic translation of *Anal. Pr.*

Regarding this translation, D. M. Dunlop remarks

---

[1] The account of Arabic studies of *Anal. Pr.* given in this section is based, in large measure, upon three sources: (1) Max Meyerhof, "Von Alexandrien nach Baghdad". *Sitzungsberichte der Preussischen Akademie der Wissenschaften* (philosophisch-historische Klasse), vol. 23 (1930). (2) August Müller, *Die Griechischen Philosophen in der Arabischen Ueberlieferung*. Halle, 1873. [Annotated translation of the important bibliography *Kitāb al-fihrist* of Ibn al-Nadīm (d. c. 995).] (3) Richard Walzer, "New Light on the Arabic Translations of Aristotle". *Oriens*, vol. 6 (1953), pp. 91–142 (reprinted in *Greek into Arabic*, Oxford, 1962).

that it "was superseded so effectually that it is only by chance that we know anything about it" (*J.R.A.S.*, 1959, p. 145).

(B) *Theodore* (c. 790–c. 850), a scholar whom we cannot identify with certainty (see Dunlop, *loc. cit.*, p. 145, footnote 3), made:

(2) An Arabic translation of *Anal. Pr.*

This work survives in a revision by Ḥunain ibn Isḥāq (see below).

(C) *Al-Kindī* (c. 805–873), the well-known philosopher, wrote:

(3) A short commentary (epitome) on *Anal. Pr.*

This has not survived.

(D) *Ḥunain ibn Isḥāq* (808–877), the famous translator, assisted by his son.

(E) *Isḥāq ibn Ḥunain* (c. 845–910/911), made:

(4) A Syriac translation of *Anal. Pr.*

This work, now lost, served as a means towards the preparation (by Ḥunain) of:

(5) An Arabic translation of *Anal. Pr.*, or rather a revision of that of "Theodore".

This translation, i.e., (5), has survived (Brockelmann, *GAL*, I, 206) as edited and supplied with copious annotations by al-Ḥasan ibn Suwār (or Ibn al-Khammār; 942–1020), and was published by A. Badawī, *Manṭiq Arisṭū*, vol. I, Cairo, 1948. Ḥunain also made:

(6) A Syriac translation of Galen's treatise "On the Number of Syllogisms".

His son Isḥāq then made:

Introduction

(7) An Arabic translation of this work.

Neither of these translations has survived.

(F) *Quwairī* (Abū Isḥāq Ibrāhīm; c. 855–c. 915), an associate of Abū Bishr Mattā ibn Yūnus, the teacher of al-Fārābī, wrote in Arabic (probably):

(8) An extensive commentary on *Anal. Pr.*

This has not survived.

(G) *Al-Dimashqī* (Abū ʿUthmān; c. 860–c. 920), an eminent physician and able translator, made (presumably from the Syriac):

(9) An Arabic translation of Porphyry's "Introduction to Categorical Syllogisms".

This work is lost.

(H) *Al-Rāzī* or "Rhazes" (865–925), the famous physician, wrote:

(10) An epitome of *Anal. Pr.* (to I, 7 only).

This work is lost.

(I) *Abū Bishr Mattā ibn Yūnus* (c. 870–c. 940), the principal teacher of al-Fārābī, and an important translator, wrote (in Arabic):

(11) A commentary on *Anal. Pr.*
(12) A treatise on conditional syllogisms.

Neither of these works has survived.

It thus appears that, by the time that al-Fārābī wrote his Short Commentary on *Prior Analytics* (say around 910), he had at his disposal in Arabic the following materials: a thoroughly reliable translation of this work (item (5)); several more or less extensive commentaries (items (3), (8)?, and (11)); and several specialized treatises on the theory of the syllogism, both categorical and hypothetical (items (6), (9), and (12)). The study of Aristotelian logic in general, and of *Anal. Pr.* in particular, had gotten well under way in an Arabic-speaking setting. However, no Arabic commentary upon (or treatise dealing with special problems of) *Anal. Pr.* made prior to al-Fārābī's *Short Commentary* has survived. It is thus our sole gauge for assessing the study of "syllogistics" during the earliest phase of Arabic logic.

8. *Al-Fārābī's Short Commentary on* Prior Analytics

That al-Fārābī wrote a "short commentary" on *Prior Analytics* has long been recognized on the basis of reports in the medieval Arabic biobibliographies, and indeed this work was thought to have survived both in medieval Hebrew translation (Steinschneider, *Al-Farabi*, pp. 30–31), and supposedly (but not in fact) in the original Arabic (Escurial; MS. 612 (Derenbourg)). This treatise has become accessible through its appearance in print, as recently as 1958, in an edition by the Turkish Orientalist Mlle Mubahat Türker,[1] who has edited it from four manuscripts preserved in Istanbul,[2] and made a Turkish translation.

In the various manuscripts and citations, al-Fārābī's treatise goes under several names: *Kitāb al-qiyās al-ṣaghīr* ("Short Book on the Syllogism"), *Kitāb al-mukhtaṣar al-ṣaghīr fī-'l-kaifiyyah al-qiyās* ("Short Compendium on the Nature of the Syllogism"), and *Kitāb al-mukhtaṣar al-ṣaghīr fī-'l-manṭiqʿ alā ṭarīqah al-mutakallimīn* ("Short Compendium on Logic in the Manner of the Mutakallimūn (= Scholastic Theologians)"). But whatever the label, what we have before us is al-Fārābī's "short commentary" (epitome) of *Prior*

---

[1] "Fārābī'nin Bazi Mantik Eserleri", *Ankara Üniversitesi Dil ve Tarih-Coğrafya Fakultesi Dergisi* (*Revue de la Faculté des Langues, d'Histoire, et de Géographie de l'Université d'Ankara*), vol. 16 (1958), pp. 165–286. Mlle Türker here edits three logical treatises of al-Fārābī, two of which had previously been edited by D. M. Dunlop (for details see N. Rescher, *Al-Fārābī: An Annotated Bibliography*, or above, pp. 13, 15) and the third of which is our commentary (text pp. 244–286, Turkish translation, pp. 214–243).

[2] For details, see pp. 180–181 of Mlle Türker's monograph.

Analytics, i.e., his handbook on the subject of syllogistics (*al-qiyās*).

As is standard with the "short commentary", such a treatise, unlike a "middle" or a "long" commentary, is less of an actual commentary on an Aristotelian treatise[3] than an elementary presentation of the "branch" of logic which had grown up around the Aristotelian treatise serving as its "canonical text". (From the standpoint of the evolution of logic *instruction*, in contrast to progress of logical scholarship, a "short commentary" is thus far more illuminating, as will become apparent from a more detailed analysis of al-Fārābī's treatise.)

9. *Analysis of Al-Fārābī's Short Commentary on* Anal. Pr.

Al-Fārābī's commentary may be divided into ten sections, whose contents are as follows:

I. *Introduction*

The aims of the work—to clarify syllogisms and inference. The treatment to follow Aristotle in the ideas, but not in language or in the choice of examples, which will be adapted to contemporary requirements.[1]

II. *Categorical Propositions*

Explanations of technical terms: premiss, subject, predicate. Types of propositions: affirmative, negative; categorical, conditional. Classification of categorical propositions. The theory of opposition. Fourfold classification of statements by epistemic status: common opinion, expert opinion, sense-knowledge, and self-evident knowledge. Transition to the syllogism.

---

[3] Indeed there are only two actual quotations from *Prior Analytics*: 275: 16–17 (quoting *Anal. Pr.* 68b10-13), and 285: 14–15 (quoting *Anal. Pr.* 69a14–16).

[1] In point of fact, the examples are generally theological in character, and apparently adapted to the discussions of the *mutakallimūn* (Muslim scholastic theologians).

III. Categorical Syllogisms

One-by-one survey of the fourteen types of valid categorical syllogisms. In the case of second- and third-figure syllogisms, an explanation of their reduction to the first figure.

IV. Conditional Syllogisms

Two principal types of conditional syllogisms: conjunctive (= hypothetical) and disjunctive. The former has two principal modes: *modus ponens* and *modus tollens*. The latter splits into several types according to the diverse character of disjunctive alternatives (e.g., exhaustive or non-exhaustive).

V. "Objecting" Syllogisms

Short examination of "objecting" syllogisms (essentially, *antilogisms*).

VI. Compound Syllogisms

An explanation of "compound" syllogisms (essentially, *enthymemes* and *sorites*) and a brief discussion of ways of putting near-syllogistic arguments into the syllogistic framework.

VII. Induction

An examination of induction: what it is and how it relates to the (categorical) syllogism. Complete vs. incomplete induction. When induction is and is not possible.

VIII. Inference by "Transfer" (i.e., Analogy)

Inference by "transfer" defined, illustrated, and related to the syllogism. "Transfer" possible in two modes, the methods of analysis and of synthesis (or a combination of the two). Causal arguments. The cognate method of "investigation" of species described and related to "transfer". All the modes of "transfer" shown reducible to the (categorical) syllogism wherever their application is clearly valid.

"Transfer" may rest upon universal premisses established by the methods of "raising" and "finding". These methods described and illustrated. Two basic approaches to the "sensory-evidence" are possible in inference by "transfer". Both of these are illustrated and carried back to the syllogism.

IX. *The "Four Principles" for Establishing Statements*

In the "syllogistic arts" apart from the demonstrative (where the pure theory of the syllogism is *applied* to matters of other than a rigidly "scientific" character), four major types of "transfer" by substitution are possible for establishing the universal premisses basic to the reasoning, namely the substitution in a judgment known to be true of (1) a universal for a universal, (2) a particular for a universal, (3) a universal for a particular, and (4) a particular for a particular (viz., "example"). All of these are analyzed in detail, particular emphasis being given to (3).

X. *Conclusion*

A brief concluding discussion; principally a plea for laxity (or "generosity") in the reception of the universal premisses basic to reasoning in the non-demonstrative "syllogistic arts".

10. *The Composition of Al-Fārābī's* Short Commentary *as Contrasted with* Anal. Pr.

It is illuminating to examine the relative allocation of space given in al-Fārābī's *Short Commentary* to the various subjects treated.

Section-Topic	Percent of the Treatise
1. Introduction	4
2. Categorical Propositions	12
3. Categorical Syllogisms	15
4. Conditional Syllogisms	8

Section-Topic	Percent of the Treatise
5. "Objecting" Syllogisms	3
6. Compound Syllogisms	7
7. Induction	6
8. "Transfer" (i.e., Analogy)	20
9. "Principles" for Establishing Statements	22
10. Conclusion	3

This tabulation brings home forcibly the fact that the logical theory of the categorical syllogism, basic in *Anal. Pr.*, is only a relatively minor factor in al-Fārābī's *Short Commentary*. Even more strikingly, the theory of modal propositions and of modal syllogisms, the central theme of *Anal. Pr.*, to which Aristotle devotes well over half of his treatise, is passed over in complete silence. (This is the case also, though less importantly, with fallacies, which Aristotle treats at some length.)

It is interesting to contrast the topical coverage of al-Fārābī's "Short Commentary" on the *Prior Analytics* with that of Averroes' *Epitome* of this work,[1] which deals only with Sections 3–6 (inclusive) of al-Fārābī's *Short Commentary* in *exactly that order*, and in much the same manner. The materials of Sections 1–2 are omitted, no doubt because they have already been dealt with in connection with earlier parts of the logical canon. Sections 7–10 disappear from view because Averroes is a more doctrinaire Aristotelian who regards these matters as insufficiently relevant to Aristotle's text. Perhaps in deference to al-Fārābī, whose logical views

---

[1] Printed in Latin translation Vol. I of Juntine edition of Aristotle, *Aristotelis Opera Cum Averrois Commentariis*, Venice, 1550 and later; now readily available in a photographic reprinting issued in Frankfurt-am-Main, 1962. The Latin version is translated from the Hebrew by Abraham de Balmes (d. 1523), a Renaissance scholar who produced Latin versions of many of Averroes' logical works, doubtless on account of the interest in this philosopher on the part of the scholars of Renaissance Italy, especially at the University of Padua. See D. M. Dunlop, "Arabic Science in the West", *Journal of the Pakistan Historical Society* (Karachi, 1961), pp. 97 ff.

Introduction 39

he holds in great esteem, Averroes devotes the conclusion of his *Epitome* to explaining his omission of these materials.[2]

Turning our perspective about, let us take note of the basis in *Anal. Pr.* of the various subjects, other than categorical syllogisms, discussed in al-Fārābī's *Short Commentary*:

Section-Topic	Basis in Anal. Pr.
4. Conditional Syllogisms	
(a) Conjunctive (Hypothetical)	I, 44[3]
(b) Disjunctive	—
5. "Objecting" Syllogisms	II, 26 (cf. 8–11)
6. Compound Syllogisms	II, 27
7. Induction	II, 23
8. "Transfer" (i.e., Analogy)	II, 25
9. "Principles" for Establishing Statements	
(a) Those involving universals	—
(b) Example	II, 24

We see at once that al-Fārābī's discussion, apart from its compact treatment of categorical syllogisms, is devoted solely and exclusively to: (i) the theory of conditional syllogisms with respect to which *Anal. Pr.* is virtually silent, apart from the "promissory note" of 50a40; and (ii) the logic of arguments which can be related to the syllogism in various ways, dealt with in the final portion of Book II of *Anal. Pr.* To this second item, some 6 percent of *Anal. Pr.*, some 60 percent of al-Fārābī's *Short Commentary* is devoted!

It appears that in al-Fārābī's time, the moulding influence upon the curriculum of logical studies of the Greek and especially the Syriac Christian Aristotelians continued to make itself felt.[4] This fact regarding the then-traditional

---

[2] See pp. 51 *verso*–52 *recto* of Vol. I of the edition cited in the preceding footnote.

[3] *Anal. Pr.* 50a40–50b2 promises a subsequent discussion of hypothetical arguments, a promise not fulfilled in Aristotle's extant works.

[4] To take just one illustration: al-Fārābī's treatment of categorical syllogisms in Section 3, for example, is astoundingly similar to that of Probha (fl. c. 480, see Section 6 above).

curriculum, I believe, partly explains why al-Fārābī's Short Commentary on Anal. Pr. is silent about modal syllogisms[5]—although these actually comprise the main topic of that work—and devotes the bulk of its effort to topics which are very much of a side issue in Anal. Pr. (This shift in focus has the effect of forcing the treatment into expansions and elaborations in the treatment of topics that lead beyond the Aristotelian basis, and is therefore not without consequences of substantive interest.) The theory of modal, and above all of apodictic syllogisms in *Prior Analytics*, and the epistemology of "scientific syllogisms" of *Posterior Analytics* to which it is preparatory, is omitted from al-Fārābī's purview in the present work. In place of Aristotle's stress upon "scientific syllogism", we find that the emphasis is put upon the "syllogistic arts", and we are given elaborate defenses of "laxity" (or "generosity") in the acceptance of syllogistic premises. It would seem that, as Section 4 of al-Fārābī's *Short Commentary* reflects the influence of the Stoic logicians, so Sections 5–6 reflect the import of the epistemological views of the Syrian theologian-logicians, with their disdain for modal syllogisms and their theologically motivated dislike of the epistemology of *Anal. Post.*

Al-Fārābī's *Short Commentary* in its turn significantly influenced the way in which later Arabic logicians conceived of the materials of their discipline. To give but one example, the section (Chapter 7) on "analytics" (*al-qiyās*) of Maimonides' (d. 1204) handbook of logical terminology[6] is clearly in

---

[5] Al-Fārābī himself of course had nothing against the modal syllogistic which, as we know, he treated extensively in his *Great Commentary on Anal. Pr.* (see Steinschneider, *Al-Farabi*, p. 37).

[6] *Maqālah fī-ṣinā'ah al-manṭiq.* See Israel Efros, *Maimonides' Treatise on Logic* (N.Y., 1938), for an edition of the Arabic original (in Hebrew characters) and three medieval Hebrew translations, together with an English translation. The Arabic text has been edited from several newly recovered manuscripts by Mubahat Türker. *Musa b. Maymūn'un "Maqāla fī ṣinā' at al-manṭiq." Review of the Institute of Islamic Studies* (Istanbul University, Edebiyat Fakultesi Yayinlari), 1960.

Introduction

the tradition of al-Fārābī, whose logical work Maimonides greatly admired. The order of the presentation, the classification of the different types of syllogisms, the technical terminology employed, the explanation of concepts, and the examples given all closely resemble their counterparts in al-Fārābī's discussion. Even the subject materials of Sections 7 and 8 (induction/"investigation" and "transfer"/analogy), omitted by Averroes, figure in Maimonides' treatment.

11. *Items of Special Interest in Al-Fārābī's Short Commentary on* Anal. Pr.

I take a part of al-Fārābī's discussion to constitute an "item of special interest" when it goes sufficiently beyond its Aristotelian starting-point to qualify as an independent contribution to logic. In some instances, e.g., in the case of conditional syllogisms, we are able to credit the development to logicians prior to al-Fārābī (the Stoics, in this instance). In other cases, the credit of innovation may possibly be due to al-Fārābī himself, although any such claim would be premature at this juncture, when the (actually quite fertile) history of logic in the millennium between Aristotle and al-Fārābī remains in such large measure unexplored.

(i) *The Epistemic Status of "Known" Statements*

Al-Fārābī gives a fourfold classification of "known" statements (249: 20–250: 11), and invokes this classification in repeated uses in the subsequent discussion. Although it has an Aristotelian basis (in the *Topica!*), this schematism goes beyond its roots in the Organon. Perhaps it derives from Stoic discussions of *lēmmata* ("accepted propositions") or from Galen.[1]

---

[1] See Ivan von Müller, "Über Galen's Werk vom wissenschaftlichen Beweis", *Abhandlungen der K. Bayerischen Akademie der Wissenschaften* (phil.-hist. Klasse), vol. 20 (München, 1897), pp. 405–478 (see pp. 453–459).

(ii) Ecthesis

Al-Fārābī expounds and uses a mode of *ecthesis* (see 253: 21–254: 8) which differs somewhat from that employed by Aristotle in *Anal. Pr.* (Aristotle's *ecthesis*, though its nature is somewhat unclear, apparently "selects out" a subspecies; al-Fārābī's is clearly extensional and "selects out" a suitable *subclass*.) In reducing categorical syllogisms of other figures to those of the first, al-Fārābī gives the preference to this mode of *ecthesis*, reversing Aristotle's preference for *reductio*.[2] A detailed comparison of al-Fārābī's treatment of first-figure reduction with that of Aristotle is given in the following tabulation:

Al-Fārābī's Treatment of Categorical Syllogisms[1]		
Number	Form	Reduction
First Figure		
1	AAA-1 (Barbara)	Self-evident
2	EAE-1 (Celarent)	,,
3	AII-1 (Darii)	,,
4	EIO-1 (Ferio)	,,
Second Figure		
5	EAE-2 (Cesare)	C to 2
6	AEE-2 (Camestres)	C to 2
7	EIO-2 (Festino)	C to 4
8	AOO-2 (Baroko)	E to 6[4]
Third Figure		
9	AAI-3 (Darapti)	C to 3
10	EAO-3 (Felapton)	C to 4
11	AII-3 (Datisi)[2]	C to 3
12	IAI-3 (Disamis)[2]	C to 3
13	EIO-3 (Ferison)[3]	C to 4
14	OAO-3 (Bokardo)[3]	E to 10[4]

[1] Al-Fārābī's treatment is in agreement with Aristotle's in *Anal. Pr.*, except as noted below. KEY: C = conversion, E = ecthesis.

[2] The discussion of *Datisi* and *Disamis* is reversed with respect to Aristotle's order of treatment.

[3] The discussion of *Ferison* and *Bokardo* is reversed with respect to Aristotle's order of treatment.

[4] Aristotle reduces *Baroko* and *Bokardo* to the first figure by *reductio*. Al-Fārābī instead employs a mode of "ecthesis".

---

[2] For a clear and compact summary of Aristotle's treatment of

Introduction

(iii) *Conditional Syllogisms*

There is no discussion of conditional syllogisms in *Anal. Pr.* (although a treatment of the hypothetical syllogism is promised). Al-Fārābī's handling of conditional syllogisms in Section 4, which closely resembles that of Boethius, is derived from ultimately Stoic sources.[3]

(iv) *"Objecting" Syllogisms*

Although al-Fārābī's discussion of "objecting" syllogisms in Section 5 is based on Aristotelian ideas (specifically *Anal. Pr.* II, 26, and cf. 8-11), it surpasses its original basis both in scope and in systematic precision.

(v) *Induction*

Al-Fārābī's treatment of induction in Section 7 also goes beyond its original (in *Anal. Pr.* II, 23) in precision of development. This holds, in particular, for his analysis of the circumstances under which induction is, or is not possible.

(vi) *"Transfer" (i.e., Analogy)*

Al-Fārābī's long discussion of inference by "transfer" in Section 8 is deserving of a special monographic study. Its materials go so far beyond its Aristotelian original (in *Anal. Pr.* II, 25) as to qualify, in effect, as an entirely fresh approach to the subject. The treatment of the methods of transfer by "analysis", by "synthesis", and by the "investigation of species" constitutes an interesting way of systematizing discussion of the subject of essentially inductive reasoning within the framework of the categorical syllogism. And the discussion on the establishment of universal premises by

---

ecthesis, see W. and M. Kneale, *The Development of Logic* (Oxford, 1962), pp. 77-78.

[3] For further details see N. Rescher, "Avicenna on the Logic of Conditional Syllogisms", *The Notre Dame Journal of Formal Logic*, vol. 4 (1963).

the methods of "raising" and "finding" deserves to be regarded as an approach to the theoretical methodology for establishing of empirical generalizations which finds virtually no successor prior to Baconian times.[4]

(vii) *The "Principles" for Establishing Statements*

Al-Fārābī's defense, in Section 9, of those "syllogistic arts", in which there are requirements for logically less rigorous methods for the establishment of premises for reasoning, is one of the most striking features of the *Short Commentary*. Al-Fārābī makes repeated pleas for laxity (or "generosity") in dispensing with "exactness" in these matters.[5] We have already dwelt upon this in the preceding section.

12. *Some Points of Mechanics*

In translating al-Fārābī's Short Commentary on *Prior Analytics*, I have adopted the course of making the translation as literal as is consistent with the production of intelligible English. (An impatient reader may sometimes feel that I have failed this latter *desideratum*.) With a text of this sort, this seems to me the only reasonable course.

Technical terms of logic are rendered by their technical English equivalents, when available.[1] If the original term functions in some technical way which might fail to be evident after translation, I have put quotes about the English word, to signal that a specialized usage is at issue.

In the case of variation in manuscript readings, I accept the reading adopted by Mlle Türker, unless noted otherwise. In a few instances, the sense seems to me to require readings

---

[4] The nature and the sources of the concept of *cause* operative in Section 8 deserve, and would repay, further study.

[5] See 282: 12 and following, and 284: 18 and following.

[1] I have not deemed it necessary to provide a glossary of technical terms, having essentially discharged this task in my translation of "The Logic-Chapter of Muḥammad ibn Aḥmad al-Khwārizmī's Encyclopedia, *Keys to the Sciences* (c. 980 A.D.)", *Archiv für Geschichte der Philosophie*, vol. 44 (1962), pp. 62–74.

Introduction 45

(always noted) which, to judge by the printed edition, have no manuscript warrant. But typesetters as well as scribes are human.

In the translation, the division into sections and into paragraphs is in most instances without manuscript warrant, and dictated by the sense of the discussion alone.² Even the division into sentences is, as any Arabist knows, in some measure arbitrary.

The marginal numbering throughout the translation gives the reference to Mlle Türker's edition, the transition from line to line being indicated by |. For grammatical reasons this division cannot but be occasionally imperfect.

It is a matter of regret to me that I was able to make no use of Mlle Türker's translation; as I know no Turkish, it is a closed book to me.

---

² The text makes several explicit references to sectional divisions: 280: 10, 280: 13, 284: 12, and 286: 2.

AL-FĀRĀBĪ'S
SHORT COMMENTARY
ON
ARISTOTLE'S
PRIOR ANALYTICS

In the Name of God, the Compassionate, the Merciful.

THE SHORT TREATISE ON THE SYLLOGISM
of
Abū Naṣr al-Fārābī

Section 1

INTRODUCTION

| Our aim in this book of ours is to show (1) what the syllogism and what inference are, (2) by what | means unknowns which we seek to know are to be discovered, and (3) how many kinds of syllogisms there are, and how | and of what each one is put together.

We shall see to it that the canons[1] which we shall lay down here | are exactly those which Aristotle contributed to the art of logic. [However,] we shall strive to | express these matters, as much as possible, by means of words familiar to people who use the Arabic language.
| We shall use for the explanation of these matters examples familiar to people of our day. For | Aristotle, when he laid down these matters in his books, expressed them by means of words customary | among the people of his language, and used examples that were familiar to and current among the people of his day. But since | the explanations of the people of this [i.e., our] language are not customary to the people of that land [i.e., Greece], and the examples of the people | of this time, which are familiar among them, are different from the examples familiar to those [people], the points which | Aristotle intended to clarify by means of these examples have become unclear to

---

[1] Al-Fārābī is fond of the Arabic loan-version (*qānūn*) of the Greek *kanōn*.

12 and not understood by the people | of our time. In consequence, many of the people of these times think that his
13 books on logic are useless, | and they have been laid aside.

When it is our aim to explain these [Aristotelian] canons,
245 we use for their clarification || examples current among the scholars of the people of our time. To follow in Aristotle's
2 footsteps | in explaining what he wrote about the canons [of inference] does not consist in using [his own] and
3 examples as though one were a follower | of his in proportion as these [expressions and examples] appear of his making.
4 This would be the action of a fool.² Rather, | to follow him is to imitate his practice as proportioned to his *intention*
5 in that action. For his aim | in [giving] these examples and words was not to restrict the educated person solely to a
6 knowledge of them alone. And he did not [intend] | that one pursue an understanding of what is in his books by those examples [of his] alone, without anything else.
7 | Rather, he intended to have people know these canons through materials which happen to be the best known
8 | to them.

Thus it is not adopting his precedent to express these matters to the people of our language by using Greek words,
9 | even though he, when he composed them [i.e., his works], expressed them in Greek. Rather, to follow him is to
10 explain what is in his book | to the people of any language by means of their accustomed words. Likewise in regard to
11 examples, to adopt his precedent is not to | limit ourselves only to what he brought forward, but to follow in his
12 footsteps in this regard is to explain | the canons found in his books to the people of every art and of every science
13 and to the scholars in every age | by means of examples which are familiar to them. For this reason, we have thought fit to discard certain examples which he gave that
14 do not lie within the experience | customary to scholars of our time, and [instead] use [examples] familiar to them.³

---

[2] I suppose *gh-b-y* for the *gh-n-y* of M. Türker's text.

[3] Note that the sole claim to novelty relates to the machinery of

15   In this book of ours we shall limit ourselves to | what is absolutely necessary with regard to the syllogism. We keep our discussion of it brief, and simplify the matters we
16 wish to treat | as much as we can.[4] Let the beginning [of this discussion] be as follows:

---

instruction. We are to suppose that the substance of logical doctrine is pure and unadulterated Aristotle.

[4] This remark characterizes the present treatise as a "short commentary".

Section 2

CATEGORICAL PROPOSITIONS

245 (i) STATEMENTS AND THEIR TYPES

17 | A *premiss* and a *judgment* (proposition) are statements in which one thing is judged about another; for example, the
18 statements "Zaid is going", | "Amr is departing", and "Man walks". Here it is judged about Zaid that he is
19 going, and he is characterized by this. | Thus *Zaid* is the [thing] characterized by going, and about which this is
20 judged; and *going* is the thing which | is judged about Zaid. The characteristic may be a noun, for example, in the state-
246 ment "Zaid is a man (human being)"; || or it may be a verb, for example, in the statement "Zaid walks" or "Zaid walked".

2 Among the verbs, some indicate past time, | e.g., in the sentence "Zaid walked"; some indicate the future, e.g., in
3 the sentence "Zaid (will) be walking"; and some | indicate the present. The verbal expression indicating the present
4 in the Arabic language is of the same structure | as that of the future, e.g., "Zaid (will) be walking". If we wish to
5 conjugate the premiss which | characterizes the noun in the three tenses, we must put into the premiss "was", "will be",
6 "there was", | "there will be", "there is now", or some such
7 thing. Thus we say "Zaid was going" | and[1] "Zaid is now going". People [i.e., logicians] call the premisses which con-
8 tain "was" and "is" | and so on *triadic premisses*, and those which do not contain such an expression they call *dyadic*.

9 | Let the characteristic be called the *predicate* and that which is characterized the *subject*. It must be known that
10 predicates | and subjects are strictly speaking the *meanings* of nouns and verbs, not the nouns and verbs [themselves].
11 Only | since it was difficult at the outset to achieve an

---

[1] I suppose *w* for the *f* of M. Türker's text.

understanding of the *meanings*, the words were substituted
in their place.² | Thus they [i.e., verbs and nouns] were
taken as though they were predicates and subjects.

Every premiss either *affirms* | one thing about another,
like the statement "Amr is going", or *denies* one thing of
another, like the statement | "Zaid is not going". And
every premiss is either categorical or conditional. | A *categorical* [statement] is one in which a judgment is affirmed
and definitely affirmed, be it affirmatively or negatively;
for example, the statements "Zaid | walks" and "Amr is
not going". A *conditional* [statement] is any which subsumes a judgment under a condition.

| Conditional [statements] either (1) maintain a conjoining
of one thing with another, as in the statement "If the sun
has risen, it is | day"—for this particle [viz., "if"], and others
like it such as "when" and "whenever", subsume the existence | of day under the rising of the sun, and makes [the
former] dependent upon the connection with it [i.e., the
latter]. Or (2) [a conditional statement] maintains the disjoining of one thing from | another or its separation from
it, as in the statement "This time is either night or it is
day". For the particle | "either", and others like it such
as "or", indicate a separation between day and night.

(ii) CLASSIFICATION OF CATEGORICAL
STATEMENTS

Categorical premisses || include (1) those whose subjects
are universal and general, as in the statement "Man is an
animal", and (2) those | whose subjects are particular things
[i.e., individuals], as in the statement "Zaid is white". A
universal is that of which there are numerous similar
instances; | a particular or individual is that of which it
is impossible that there should be two instances of the
original, like Zaid and Amr.

| And similarly with the predicates of premisses. Some

---

² Is this to be construed as an assertion (the first) of the distinction
between *suppositio materialis* and *suppositio formalis*?

are universals, as in the statement "Zaid is a man"—for *man* is a universal which is [here] predicated of Zaid, Zaid being a particular [individual]. And some are particulars, as in the statement "This sitting person is Zaid".

Premises whose subjects are universals include [principally] those which attach to the subject something which indicates that the judgment is partial [particular] or [that it is] total [universal], and this both in denial and in assertion. This [quantity] is indicated by expressions such as "every" and "a certain", or "some" and "not a single", and "not every". These particles are called *quantity-indicators*.[3]

The term "every" is used to make an assertion about the whole [i.e., all], and "some" or "a certain" to make an affirmation (assertion) about some [i.e., a part]. "Not a single" is used to make a denial about the whole, and "not every" is used to make a denial about some [i.e., a part].

An affirmation which attaches to a subject something which indicates that the predicate is asserted of the whole [subject]—as in the statement "Every man is an animal"— is an *affirmative universal*. That [statement] which attaches to its subject something which indicates that the predicate is asserted about *some* of it [viz., the subject]—like[4] the statements "A certain man is white", or "Some man is white", or the like— is called an *affirmative particular*. As to a negative [statement] which attaches to its subject something which indicates that the predicate is denied about the whole [subject]—like the statement "No single man is a bird"—it is called a *negative universal*. And the negative which attaches to its subject something that indicates that the predicate is denied about some of it [viz., the subject]—like the statements "Not every man is white" or "Some persons are not white" or "Some man is not white"—is called a *negative particular*.

---

[3] Sing. *sūr*, literally *delimitant*.
[4] I suppose *ka* for the *fa* of M. Türker's text.

(iii) THE OPPOSITION OF CATEGORICAL STATEMENTS

| Affirmations and negations are either opposed or not. An affirmative | and a negative [statement] are opposed only if they meet certain conditions, namely: (1) that | their subjects be one and the same thing, (2) and their predicates likewise, and (3) that the time || at which the predicate is affirmed of the subject [in the statement] be exactly the same time as that at which the predicate is denied of | the subject [in the other], and (4) that the state in which the subject is to be found as subject of the predicate in the affirmation | is exactly the same as the state in which this subject is to be found in the negation, and (5) that the state in which the predicate is to be found | as predicate of the subject in the affirmation is exactly the same state in which it is to be found | in the negation. If a single one of these five conditions is lacking, then the affirmation | and the negation will not be opposed. The meaning of "opposite" is that two things do not accord with one another. The other conditions which are thought | to be additional to these are actually included within the group we have enumerated.

Take for example the statement | "Zaid the clerk had an eye-ailment yesterday". This judgment affirms an ailment of Zaid. It | is to be construed with respect to a certain state and at an accomplished past time. Thus the negative which opposes it is *not* the statement "Zaid | is not ill", but rather the statement "Zaid the clerk did not have an eye-ailment yesterday". | Likewise when we say "The negro is a white man" then the opposite negative is that we say "The negro | is not a white man", and *not* that we say "The negro is not white". So much for the conditions | which govern the opposition of affirmations and negations.

(iv) CLASSIFICATION OF OPPOSITES

| Mutually opposed premisses are of several kinds: (1) Some have subjects that are particulars, like the

statements "Zaid is white" | and "Zaid is not white". These are called *particularized opposites*, and they divide truth | and falsity between them always and in every case; namely if either one of them is true concerning any | matter, the other must be false—they never agree with one another with respect to truth or falsity alone.

| (2) Some have subjects that are universals. These are called *generalized opposites*.

(2a) Some of | these attach to the [common] subject of both opposites a quantity-indicator which indicates that the judgment applies generally | to the whole subject. The two [statements of this sort] are called *contraries*. For example, the statements "Every man is an animal" and "Not a single man || is an animal". Two such [statements] divide truth and falsity between them sometimes: namely in matters of necessity | and impossibility, as with the statements, "Every man is an animal" and "Not a single man is an animal"; or, "Every man | flies" and "Not a single man flies".[5] But sometimes they are both false together, namely in matters of possibility, | as, for example, the statements, "Every man is white" and "Not a single man is white".[6]

| (2b) Some connect to the [common] subjects of both opposites a particular quantity-indicator to indicate that the judgment | pertains [only] to *some* of the subject. For example, the statements "Some men are white", and "Not every man is white". These | are called *subcontraries*.[7] These divide truth and falsity between them sometimes, namely | in matters of necessity and of impossibility,[8] as with

---

[5] If an X *must* be a Y, or if it *cannot possibly* be a Y, then the statements "All X is Y" and "No X is Y" will clearly "divide truth and falsity between them".

[6] If an X *may or may not* be a Y, then "All X is Y" and "No X is Y" will both be false (assuming the modality of possibility to be so construed that "A's may possibly be B's" entails "Some A is B").

[7] Literally: *that which is under the contraries*.

[8] The text reads "possible" for "impossible"; we must suppose a missing *ghair*.

the statements, "Some men are animals" and "Not every man | is an animal", or "Some man flies" and "Not every man flies".[9] But sometimes they are both true together, namely | in [matters of] possibility as, for example, the statements, "Some man is white" and "Not every man is white".[10]

(2c) Some of them [i.e., some generalized opposites] | connect to the subject of one of the two opposites a universal quantity-indicator and to [that of] the other a particular quantity-indicator. These are called | *contradictories*. (2ci) Some contraries connect a universal quantity-indicator to the subject of an affirmation and a particular [quantity-indicator] | to the subject of a negation; for example, the statements "Every man is an animal" and "Not every man is an animal". (2cii) Some of them [i.e., some contraries] | connect to the subject of an affirmation a particular quantity-indicator, and to the subject of a negation | a universal quantity-indicator; e.g., the statements "Some man is an animal" and "Not a single man is an animal". These | two kinds of contraries divide truth and falsity between them always and in every | case.

(2d) Some of them [i.e., some contraries] do not connect to the subject of one of two opposites any quantity-indicator at all; e.g., the statements | "Man is an animal" and "Man is not an animal". These are called "indeterminates". Their status in respect to truth | and falsity is the same as with the subcontraries.

(v) THE EPISTEMIC STATUS OF STATEMENTS

| Some premisses are known to be factual and some not known to be factual. | A [premiss] known to be factual is

---

[9] If an X *must* be a Y, or if it *cannot possibly* be a Y, then the statements "Some X is Y" and "Some X is not Y" will clearly "divide truth and falsity between them".

[10] If an X *may or may not* be a Y, then the statements "Some X is Y" and "Some X is not Y" will both be true (given the supposition of footnote 6 above with respect to the modality of possibility).

one regarding which we have ascertained it as true either that it is thus-and-so or that it is not thus-and-so. A [premiss] not | known [to be factual] is one regarding which we have not arrived at the definite conclusion either that it is thus-and-so or that it is not thus-and-so.

|| A [premiss] known [to be factual] is [either] known by a syllogism, or it is not arrived at by a syllogism. | Those [premisses] which we have ascertained [to be factual], but whose truth is not derived from a syllogism, are of four kinds: | (1) received, (2) well-known, (3) sensory, and (4) intellectual by nature.

(1) A *received* [known statement] is any statement | which is received by a single mortal or by a collection of mortals.

(2) A *well-known* [known statement] is any statement which is | universally acknowledged by all men or the majority of men, or by [all] scholars and men of intelligence or the majority | of these, when no one takes exception to it. A [statement] well known among the experts of some field is one that is | accepted by [all or most of] the experts of this field, with no one to oppose it, neither amongst them nor amongst others.

| (3) A *sensory* [known statement] is one like "Zaid is walking".

(4) The [known statements] *intellectual by nature* are universal premisses which man finds | to be self-evident, as though they were natural to the intellect, or which man is certain from his first creation without understanding how he arrived | at it. For example the statements, "Every three[11] is an odd number" and "Every four is an even number".[12]

---

[11] I suppose *th-l-'-th-h* for the *th-l-th-l-h* of M. Türker's text.

[12] Al-Fārābī thus has a fourfold classification of the epistemic status of "known statements" not arrived at by syllogistic means, viz., common opinion, expert opinion, sense-knowledge, and self-evident knowledge. (Cp. *Anal. Pr.* 24a23, *Topica* 100a29, 101a12, 104a7, and 105a36.) Inferential knowledge arrived at syllogistically will, as we shall shortly see, be carried back to these four categories.

11 | The [only known statements] to be added to these four [kinds] are those which can be known from a syllogism.¹³

250 (vi) SYLLOGISM

12 | A syllogism is a body of discourse made up of premises so constituted that if conjoined there follows from them,
13 essentially | and not by accident, some other, different thing as the outcome. Whatever knowledge is arrived at
14 by the syllogism is called | the *conclusion* and the *consequence*.

A syllogism is composed of premises which are known
15 in one of these "four ways". | It may also be composed of premises which are conclusions of other syllogisms whose
16 premises reduce | to knowledge in one of these "four ways".

A syllogism is, at a minimum, composed of two premises
17 | sharing one common "part".¹⁴ Syllogisms may be com-
18 posed of conditional premises and of | categorical premises.

---

¹³ *Ergo* induction, example, and all other ways of securing knowledge must, as we shall see, be reduced to the syllogism.

¹⁴ Here, and frequently (though not invariably) throughout the text, al-Fārābī uses the word *part* (*juz'*) as a neutral word which can stand for either the *term* (properly *ḥadd*) of a categorical proposition, or the component proposition of a conditional proposition.

Section 3

CATEGORICAL SYLLOGISMS

| The [types of] categorical syllogisms are fourteen in number.

Syllogism 1

The first of them is composed as follows, arising when we assume | that we are given two known premises, each belonging to one of the "four ways", [as follows]: "Every corporeal substance (C) || is composite (K), and Every K is created (R), so it is inescapably necessary that Every C | is R".[1] This is the first syllogism. It is composed of two premises that are universal[2] affirmative, | and share in common one "part" (term)[3] namely the composite (K). The composite (K) is shared by the two premises together in such a way | as to be subject in one of them and predicate in the other. The term that is shared is called | the *middle term*. The other two terms are called the *extremes*[4] of the syllogism. And the premiss in which one finds | the middle term as subject, that is the major premiss;[5]

---

[1] For the reader's convenience I use literal abbreviations to make the logic of the discussion more perspicuous. In al-Fārābī's text these do not occur: everything is written out in full.

[2] Here, and throughout the present text, *'āmiyy* is used for "universal", instead of the term *kulliyy* standard in later Arabic usage.

[3] See footnote 14 of Section 2 above.

[4] The word *ṭaraf* = "extreme term (of a syllogism)" is characteristic of 9th-century Arabic logical texts, but rare thereafter.

[5] Note the procedure of identifying (i.e., discriminating between) the major and the minor premiss on basis of the position of occurrence (as subject or predicate) of the middle term. It is clear that this procedure, adequate to first-figure syllogisms, will not serve for figures two and three.

Al-Fārābī's Short Commentary 61

7 while that in which one finds | the middle term as predicate is the minor premiss.⁶

251 *Syllogism 2*

8 | The second syllogism [is as follows]: "Every corporeal substance (C) is composite (K), and no single K is eternal
9 (E), so it is necessary | by this that no single C is E". Here
10 the middle term is K. This syllogism is composed of | two premisses: its minor is affirmative universal, its major is negative universal; and the conclusion is negative universal.⁷

251 *Syllogism 3*

11 | The third syllogism [is as follows]: "Some existing thing (X) is composite (K), and Every K is created (R), so it is
12 necessary that | some X is R". This [syllogism] consists of two premisses—its minor is affirmative particular, and its
13 major | is affirmative universal. Its middle term is K. The conclusion is affirmative particular.⁸

251 *Syllogism 4*

14 | The fourth syllogism [is as follows]: "Some existing thing (X) is composite (K), and no single K is eternal (E), so it is
15 necessary | by this that some X is not E". ⁹ This syllogism

⁶ The first syllogism is AAA-1 (Barbara):

(m): All C is K
(M): All K is R
(C): All C is R

The ordering *minor: major: conclusion* is standard throughout al-Fārābī's discussion of categorical syllogisms.

⁷ The second syllogism is EAE-1 (Celarent):

(m): All C is K
(M): No K is E
(C): No C is E

⁸ The third syllogism is AII-1 (Darii):

(m): Some X is K
(M): All K is R
(C): Some X is R

⁹ Literally: *that Not every X is E*. Al-Fārābī frequently formulates O-propositions in this way.

16 consists of two premises; | its minor is affirmative particular, and its major is negative universal. Its conclusion is negative particular.[10]

17 It is clear | with regard to these [first] four syllogisms that their middle term is the subject of one of the two
18 extremes | and the predicate of the other. Syllogisms in which the middle term is ordered[11] between the two ex-
19 tremes | in this ordering are called syllogisms of the *first figure*.[12]

These [first] four syllogisms, are such that it is self-
20 evident | that they yield the conclusions that have been mentioned. When this is the case with syllogisms, they
21 are | [called] *perfect syllogisms*. Except for these [four], it
252 cannot be self-evident that what is given || as their conclusions is derived with necessity from them [i.e., from two premisses], but this is shown only by reducing them to these four perfect [syllogisms].[13]

252   *Syllogism 5*
2 | The fifth syllogism [is as follows]: "Every corporeal sub-

[10] The fourth syllogism is EIO-1 (Ferio):

    (m): Some X is K
    (M): No K is E
    ―――――――――――
    (C): Some X is not E

[11] I suppose *y-r-t-b* for the *y-r-b-t* of M. Türker's text. Here "ordering" is a technical term to stand for the occurrence-pattern of the terms in the premisses of a syllogism.

[12] Note that the first figure is defined in terms of the position of occurrence (as subject or predicate) in the premisses of the middle term. This procedure can (and indeed will in the present text) be extended to furnish definitions of the two other syllogistic figures. However—as was remarked in footnote 5 above—this approach does not suffice, in second- and third-figure syllogisms, for differentiating between the major and minor premiss. Here an additional resort (namely to the conclusion) will prove to be necessary.

[13] Only the first four syllogisms are "perfect" and "self-evident" in that their very structure is claimed of itself to furnish their justification. All other syllogisms must, as with Aristotle, be justified (by some process of reduction) in terms of these four.

stance (C) is composite (K), and no single eternal thing (E) is K, so it is necessary from this that no single C is E". The shared [term] in the two premisses of this syllogism is K, which is predicated of the two remaining extreme terms. The minor premiss here is that whose subject is the subject of the conclusion, namely the statement "Every C is K". The major premiss is that whose subject is the predicate of the conclusion, namely the statement "No single E is K".[14]

When syllogisms are such that the middle term is arranged within them in this arrangement, namely when it is predicated of both the extremes, then these are called syllogisms of the *second figure*. The major premiss in this [fifth] syllogism is negative universal, and the minor is affirmative universal.[15]

[In] this syllogism it is not self-evident that what is given as its conclusion is derived from it as it is supposed to be. Rather, it needs for its being-evident some other thing to render necessary that [conclusion] which is given.

The proof of this is [given by the fact] that the statement "No single E is K" already includes the statement "No single K is E".

This state of affairs holds for every negative universal [proposition], like the statement "No single man is a thing that flies", which already includes [the statement] "No single thing that flies is a man". For if we assert either one of these we have [in effect] already [*ipso facto*] asserted the other. If either of them is true, the other is true [also],

[14] The fifth syllogism is EAE-2 (Cesare):

(m): All C is K
(M): No E is K
(C): No C is E

[15] Note that the discrimination between the major and minor premiss is here based, in effect, on a reference to the conclusion—the major being that premiss which contains the predicate of the conclusion, and the minor that premiss which contains the subject of the conclusion.

15 because a negative universal [proposition] | becomes true through the truth of its converse; and when its converse is not true, it itself is not true. For whenever we deny a thing
16 of one kind about | everything whatever of a second kind, then we also have thereby denied this thing of the second kind about everything of the first kind. Thus if it be the
17 case that | "No single man flies" then it is necessary that not a single thing that flies is a man, because if there were
18 | a man among the things that fly, then this thing would be a man that flies, and then it could not possibly be correct
19 to say | that "No single man flies". If there is not in the group of things that fly a man, then when we wished
20 | that truth be told us [we could be told] "No single man is a thing that flies". For it would then necessarily
21 follow that there be a thing | that is a flying man. Consequently, if we assert one of these two statements [namely: "No man is a thing that flies"—"No thing that flies is a man"] then it is exactly as though we had asserted the other.[16]

Now that our statement "No single E is K" is just of this
253 sort. || Thus when we have asserted it, we have [thereby] also[17] asserted "No single K is E". But we already have
2 | "Every C is K" [so that the required conclusion can be had by the second syllogism].

It follows that the composition of the fifth syllogism
3 already includes the composition | of the second syllogism. Thus the force of this [fifth] composition is exactly like the force of that [i.e., the second]. Thus whatever is rendered necessary by the former is rendered necessary by
4 | the latter, by virtue of this identity.[18]

[16] It is worthy of remark that al-Fārābī takes time out here—i.e., in the discussion of syllogisms—to justify the convertibility of an E-proposition. It is odd that this is argued rather than pre-supposed *in the present context*, although it does belong to the subject of "analytics" already in the treatise of Probus, and indeed in *Anal. Pr.* (see any index).

[17] I suppose f-q-d for the q-q-d of M. Türker's text.

[18] The fifth syllogism (EAE-2, Cesare) is reduced to the second

Syllogism 6

| The sixth [syllogism], the second of the second figure, [is as follows]: "No single corporeal substance (C) is uncreated (U), | and every eternal thing (E) is U, so it follows that no single C | is E". This [syllogism] consists of two premisses: its minor is negative universal, | and its major is affirmative universal. The conclusion drawn is negative universal.[19]

As regards its derivation [the following account is to be given]. The statement "No single C | is U" already includes in it [the statement] "No U is C". | But "Every E is U" has already been given. We thus arrive, in this way, at the composition of the second syllogism | by which it is thus established that "No single E is C". But if *this* [i.e., "No E is C"] is established, so also is its converse, namely | "No single C is E".[20]

Syllogism 7

| The seventh [syllogism], the third of the second [figure], is as follows: "Some existing thing (X) is composite (K), and no single eternal thing (E) | is K, so it follows that some X is not E". This [syllogism] has two premisses: | its minor is affirmative particular, and its major is negative universal. It yields [as conclusion] a negative particular.[21]

(EAE-1, Celarent) by conversion of the major premiss. This agrees with Aristotle's procedure in *Anal. Pr.*

[19] The sixth syllogism is AEE-2 (Camestres):

$$\begin{array}{l}(m):\text{ No C is U}\\(M):\text{ All E is U}\\\hline(C):\text{ No C is E}\end{array}$$

[20] The sixth syllogism (AEE-2, Camestres) is reduced to the second syllogism (EAE-1, Celarent) by converting *both* the minor premiss *and* the conclusion. This agrees with Aristotle's procedure in *Anal. Pr.*

[21] The seventh syllogism is EIO-2 (Festino):

$$\begin{array}{l}(m):\text{ Some X is K}\\(M):\text{ No E is K}\\\hline(C):\text{ Some X is not E}\end{array}$$

66   *Al-Fārābī's Short Commentary*

16 | As regards its derivation [the following account is to be given]. When we claim "No single E is K" this already
17   includes in it [the statement] "No single K | is E". But we have already been given "Some X is K". Thus this [syllogism] is reduced to the composition of the fourth [syllogism].
18   Consequently there follows | from this [i.e., the seventh syllogism] just what follows from the fourth [syllogism], namely "Some X is not E".[22]

253   *Syllogism* 8

19 | The eighth [syllogism], the fourth of the second [figure], [is as follows]: "Some existing thing (X) is not corporeal
20   (C) and every moving thing (M) | is C, so it follows that some X is not M".[22a] This [syllogism] is composed of two premises.
21   Its minor | is negative particular, and its major is affirmative universal. The conclusion is negative particular.[23]

As regards its derivation [the following account is to be
22   given]. If it be the case that | "Some X is not C" then we have already arrived at the statement "A part of the X's
254 is not || C". This shows that C is removed from the totality
2   of this part of the X's. Now if one designates | this part [of the X's] by some special name—for example, "the part P"—one arrives at the statement "No single (X of) part P
3 | is C".[24] But we have already been given "Every M is C". Thus we arrive at the composition of the sixth syllogism.[25]

[22] The seventh syllogism (EIO-2, Festino) is reduced to the fourth (EIO-1, Ferio) by converting the major premiss. This agrees with Aristotle's procedure in *Anal. Pr.*

[22a] Literally: *that not every X is M.*

[23] The eighth syllogism is AOO-2 (Baroko):

(m): Some X is not C
(M): All M is C
───────────────
(C): Some X is not M

[24] Al-Fārābī treats the O-proposition, "Some X is not Y", as equivalent (intersubstitutable) with the E-proposition, "No X-of-part-P is Y".

[25] In view of the equivalence mentioned in the preceding footnote,

on Aristotle's 'Prior Analytics'

4 | But we have already shown with respect to this [sixth]
5 syllogism that it includes the second. | Therefore it necessarily follows that "No single [X of] part P is M". But P
6 is a part of the X's—so that a part of the X's | is not M, in other words "Not all X is M" [i.e., "Some X is not M"], which is just what was to be shown.
7 This [revised argument] yields | the conclusion of the eighth [syllogism]; we have thus shown that the eighth [syllogism] is reduced to the second, through the mediation of the sixth (syllogism) between these two.
8 | This method by which we have reduced the eighth [syllogism] to the second is called *ecthesis*.[26] And the method
9 by which | we have reduced the others [i.e., syllogisms] [to the first figure] is the method of conversion.

These four syllogisms [numbers five through eight] are
10 [the valid syllogisms of] | the second figure.

---

the eighth syllogism (AOO-2; Baroko) becomes:

(m): No X-of-part-P is C
(M): All M is C
―――――――――――――――――
(C): No X-of-part-P is M

This is validated as a syllogism of the sixth kind (AEE-2, Camestres). The conclusion may then be re-translated as "Some X is not M". Al-Fārābī takes this procedure to represent Aristotle's *ecthesis* (*al-iftirāḍ*).

[26] *Ecthesis* = *al-iftirāḍ*. So far as I know, this logical use of the term is unique with al-Fārābī. It is used very differently by Avicenna. (See A. M. Goichon's *Lexique de la Langue Philosophique d'Ibn Sīnā* (p. 269).) However, as Prof. D. M. Dunlop suggests in correspondence: "Should not *al-iftiraḍ* of the text be read as *al-iftirād*, or perhaps better *al-ifrād*, from the common root f-r-d (not f-r-$ḍ$) in the sense of 'isolate, set apart'?" This eminently plausible supposition will doubtless find support as other logical texts come to light; in our text the term is a *hapax legomenon*.

Aristotle reduces Baroko by *reductio*, and not *ecthesis*. However, it deserves note that ecthesis, as used by Aristotle, corresponds with al-Fārābī's conception of the process, except that Aristotle conceives of the process in intensional terms (selecting a subspecies of a species) while al-Fārābī conceives of it in extensional terms (selecting a subset of a set).

68   *Al-Fārābī's Short Commentary*

Syllogism 9

| The ninth syllogism, the first of the third [figure], [is as follows]: "Every moved thing (M) is created (R), and | every M is corporeal (C), so it is necessary from this that some R is C". This [syllogism] | is composed of two premisses. Its minor is affirmative universal, and likewise its major. The middle term | in the two [premisses] is M, which is the subject of both extremes. The major term is C, and the minor is R.[27]

Every | syllogism which is such that its middle term is the subject of both extremes together is *ipso facto* called a syllogism | of the *third figure*.[28]

This [ninth] syllogism is the first of the syllogisms of this [third] figure. Its conclusion is affirmative | particular.

As regards its derivative [the following account is to be given]. The statement "Every M is R" already includes [the statement] "Some R | is M".

This is so because if we wish that truth be told us [when it is said that] "Every M is R", then it must necessarily be the case | that there be among the R's something that is an M. For if there were not among the R's anything that is an M, | one would arrive at [the conclusion] "No single R is M" which is negative universal, and thus includes its converse, | which converse is "No single M is R". But we have already been given "Every M is R". | Consequently it follows that if there is not among the R's anything that is M, then there is not any M || that is an R. Therefore it follows that if it be true that "Every M is R", this [state-

---

[27] The ninth syllogism is AAI-3 (Darapti):

(m): All M is R
(M): All M is C
―――――――――――
(C): Some R is C

[28] The third figure is defined, as was the first and second, in terms of the position of occurrence (as subject or predicate) in the premisses of the middle term. This means that the major and minor premisses (and/or terms) must be discriminated with reference to the conclusion, as with the second figure (see footnote 12 above).

ment] includes in it of necessity that it be [the case that] "Some R is a M".²⁹

[If "Every M is R",] it is not necessary that "Every R is M"; | otherwise the affirmative universal [statement] would entail its universal converse. For it would follow that if it were that "Every | man is an animal", then it would be that "Every animal is a man", but this is erroneous. Thus it is correct that an affirmative | universal includes of necessity only its particular converse [i.e., its converse "by limitation"], and not its universal converse [i.e., its strict converse].

| Therefore it is correct that the statement "Every M is R" already includes in it the statement "Some R | is M". But we have already been given "Every M is C". Thus the ninth [syllogism] reduces to the third [syllogism]: | therefore it [i.e., the ninth] yields as a conclusion what that one [viz., the third] yields as a conclusion, namely the statement "Some R is C".³⁰

Syllogism 10

| The tenth [syllogism], the second of the third [figure], [is as follows]: "Every eternal thing (E) is active (A), and no single E is corporeal (C), | so it is necessary by this that some A is not C".³¹ This [syllogism] is composed of two premisses: The minor being affirmative universal | and the major being negative universal. It yields a negative particular [conclusion].³²,³³

---

²⁹ It deserves remark that the present discussion enters into a justification of conversion by limitation of an A-proposition. Compare footnote 16 above.

³⁰ The ninth syllogism (AAI-3, Darapti) is reduced to the third (AII-1, Darii) by conversion by limitation of the minor premiss. This accords with Aristotle's procedure in *Anal. Pr.*

³¹ Literally: *that not every A is C.*

³² The tenth syllogism is EAO-3 (Felapton):

(m): All E is A
(M): No E is C
———————
(C): Some A is not C

The tenth syllogism (EAO-3, Felapton) is reduced to the fourth

70   *Al-Fārābī's Short Commentary*

As for its derivation [the following account is to be given]:
12 The statement "Every E | is A" includes within itself [the statement] "Some A is E". But we have already been given
13 "No single E is C". | Therefore [this syllogism] is reduced to the fourth syllogism. Consequently there is necessitated by this [i.e., the tenth] syllogism what is necessary from that
14 one [i.e., the fourth], namely that some | among the A's are not C's. Thus it is not correct that every A is C, [i.e., we have that "Some A is not C"].[34]

255   *Syllogism* 11
15 | The eleventh [syllogism], the third of the third [figure], [is as follows]: "Some corporeal substance (C) is active (A),
16 and every | C is composite (K), so it is necessary from this
17 that some A is K." This [syllogism] | is composed of two premisses: its major is affirmative universal and its minor
18 is affirmative particular. | It yields [as conclusion] an affirmative particular.[35]

As regards its derivation [the following account is to be given]. The statement "Some C is A" includes within itself
19 | [the statement] "Some A is C".

For if it is true that some C's are A's, then it is necessary
20 that there is something among the | A's that is a C, for if there were not any A in the C's, it would result that "No
256 single A is C".[36] || But this [statement] is negative universal,

---

(EIO-1, Ferio) by conversion by limitation of the minor premiss. This agrees with Aristotle's procedure in *Anal. Pr.*

[33] Al-Fārābī *reverses* Aristotle's ordering by treating Felapton *before* Datisi.

[34] The tenth syllogism (EAO-3, Felapton) is reduced to the fourth syllogism (EIO-1, Ferio) by conversion by limitation of the minor premiss. This agrees with Aristotle's procedure in *Anal. Pr.*

[35] The eleventh syllogism is AII-3 (Datisi):

(m): Some C is A
(M): All C is K
(C): Some A is K

[36] Note that *opposition* relations are assumed to be known from Section 2 above.

and thus includes in itself [its converse, namely] "No single
C is A"; and so it would not be true that | there is any C
that is A. Therefore it is correct that if "Some C is A"
is true, then "Some A is C" is also true.³⁷

Now we have already been given | "Every C is K". Thus
[the eleventh syllogism] is reduced to the third syllogism.
Therefore it necessarily follows [by the third syllogism] that
"Some A is K". But this | is what was given us as the
conclusion of the eleventh syllogism.³⁸

Syllogism 12

| The twelfth [syllogism], the fourth of the third [figure], [is
as follows]: "Every corporeal substance (C) is created (R),
and some C | is moved (M), therefore it is necessary from
this that some R is M". This [syllogism] has as its major
an affirmative | particular, and as its minor an affirmative
universal. It yields [as conclusion] an affirmative particular.³⁹

As regards its derivation [the following account is to be
given]: The statement "Some C | is M" includes in itself [the
statement] "Some M is C". But we have already been given
"Every C is R". Therefore we have reduced [the premises]
| to [those of] the third syllogism; so that it is necessitated

---

³⁷ Again the discussion is diverted to justify a conversion, this time
of an I-statement. Note the complex process by which this is accomplished:
    (1) We are given "Some C is A".
    (2) To demonstrate that "Some A is C" we assume its contradictory "No A is C" and proceed by *reductio ad absurdum*.
    (3) We convert "No A is C" to "No C is A", which contradicts (1) above. Q.E.D.

³⁸ The eleventh syllogism (AII-3, Datisi) is reduced to the third syllogism (AII-1, Darii) by conversion of the minor premiss. This agrees with Aristotle's procedure in *Anal. Pr.*

³⁹ The twelfth syllogism is IAI-3 (Disamis):
    (m): All C is R
    (M): Some C is M

    (C): Some R is M

by them that "Some M is R". But in *this* [statement] is included [the statement "Some R is M". | And this is what was given us as the conclusion of the twelfth syllogism.⁴⁰

Syllogism 13

| The thirteenth [syllogism], the fifth of the third [figure], is as follows: "Some corporeal substance (C) is active (A), | and no single C is eternal (E), therefore it is necessary from this that some A is not E". ⁴¹ The major [premiss] | of this syllogism is negative universal and its minor is affirmative particular. It yields [as conclusion] a negative particular.⁴²,⁴³

As regards | its derivation [the following account is to be given]. The statement "Some C is A" includes in itself the statement "Some A is C". But we have already been given | "No single C is E". Thus [the premises of this thirteenth syllogism] reduce to those of the fourth syllogism. Consequently, it necessarily follows that "Some A is not | E".⁴⁴,⁴⁵

Syllogism 14

| The fourteenth [syllogism], the sixth of the third [figure], [is as follows]: "Every corporeal substance (C) is created (R) | and some C is not moved (M), so it is necessary from

---

⁴⁰ The twelfth syllogism (IAI-3, Disamis) is reduced to the third syllogism (AII-1, Darii) by converting both the major premiss and the conclusion. This agrees with Aristotle's procedure in *Anal. Pr.*

⁴¹ Literally: *that not every A is E.*

⁴² The thirteenth syllogism is EIO-3 (Ferison):

(m): Some C is A
(M): No C is E
(C): Some A is not E

⁴³ Al-Fārābī reverses Aristotle's ordering by treating Ferison before Bokardo.

⁴⁴ Literally: *that not every A is E.*

⁴⁵ The thirteenth syllogism (EIO-3, Ferison) is reduced to the fourth syllogism (EIO-1, Ferio) by conversion of the minor premiss. This agrees with Aristotle's procedure in *Anal. Pr.*

this that some R is not M". Thus the major [premiss]
19 | of this syllogism is of negative particular [form], and its
minor is affirmative universal. Its conclusion is negative
particular.[46]
20 | As regards its derivation [the following account is to be
given]: if it be given us that "Some C is not M" we arrive at
257 [the consequence that] some of the C's are not || M's. It
is evident that the entirety of this part (of C) is not M,
2 and that no single thing belonging to this part (of C) | is M.
Therefore if we take this part (of C)—let it be the mountains
[= the part P]—then [the situation] is as follows: No
3 | single P is M. But we already have "Every C is R", and P
4 is (*ex hypothesi*) [a part of] C; so that we arrive at: | Every
P is R, and no single P is M. Therefore we have reduced
[this syllogism] to the tenth syllogism. Therefore it is
5 necessary by this [pair of premisses] that | "Some R is not
M". But this is what was given us as the conclusion of the
fourteenth [syllogism].[47]
6 | This completes [enumeration of] the entire collection of
categorical syllogisms.

[46] The fourteenth syllogism is OAO-3 (Bokardo):

(m): All C is R
(M): Some C is not M

(C): Some R is not M

[47] As in the derivation of the fourteenth syllogism above (OAO-3, Bokardo), al-Fārābī treats the O-proposition "Some X is not Y" as equivalent with the E-proposition "No X-of-part-P is Y". Further, the A-proposition "All X is Y" clearly yields "All X-of-part-P is Y", for any part P.
Thus the premisses of the foregoing syllogism yield:

(m): All C-of-part-P is R
(M): No C-of-part-P is M

which lead to the conclusion, "Some R is not M" by the tenth syllogism (EAO-3, Felapton). Q.E.D.
This reduction procedure, with a use of ecthesis, is a departure from Aristotle's procedure in *Anal. Pr.*, where OAO-3 is reduced to AAA-1 by *reductio ad absurdum*. But Aristotle recognizes the applicability of *ecthesis* in this case (*Anal. Pr.* 28b20-21).

Section 4

CONDITIONAL SYLLOGISMS

257
7 Let us now speak about conditional syllogisms. | Every conditional syllogism is also composed of two premisses:
8 the major [premiss] being a conditional [statement], | and the minor a categorical [statement]. [There are two types of conditional syllogisms.]¹

257 (i) CONJUNCTIVE CONDITIONAL SYLLOGISMS

The first of the two [types of conditional syllogisms] is called a *conjunctive* conditional. This [also] can be of two kinds:

257 (a) *Affirmative Mode* (*Modus Ponens*)
9 | The first of the two [kinds of conjunctive conditional syllogism] is as follows: "If the world is originated, then it has a creator; but the world is originated; therefore it
10 follows by this | that the world has a creator".²

The major of the two premisses of this syllogism is the
11 statement: "If | the world is originated, then it has a

---

¹ In the present discussion of conditional syllogisms, al-Fārābī presupposes the following classification of such syllogisms:
  (i) Conjunctive Conditional Syllogisms [= our "hypothetical syllogisms"]
    (a) Affirmative mode [= our *Modus Ponens*]
    (b) Negative mode [= our *Modus Tollens*]
  (ii) Disjunctive Conditional Syllogisms [= our "disjunctive syllogisms"].

² Thus the first kind of conjunctive conditional syllogism (viz., its affirmative mode) takes the form:

$$\frac{\text{If P then Q}}{\therefore Q}\; P$$

This is the *modus ponens* of the Latin logicians.

creator". This [premiss] is the conditional one of the two. This premiss alone is composed of two statements, of which
12 the first is | "The world is originated", and the other is "The world has a creator", which is connected[3] with the former
13 by a conditional [connection], namely by | the particle "If it be [that X, then Y]". Thus a conditional link relates
14 the second statement to the first, namely a | particle which indicates a link of the statement "[The world has] a creator" with the statement "The world is originated". And the
15 same | would be the case with [other] particles that are of this general kind, like "If it be that [X, then Y]" or "Whatever [is X, will be Y]" or "Whenever [X, then Y]", and others like them.
16 | The first [part of a conditional statement] is called the *antecedent* (protasis), and this [in the foregoing example] is the statement "If the world is originated". The second [part of a conditional statement] is called the *consequent* (apodasis), and this [in the example] is the statement:
17 | "The world has a creator". Thus a conditional [statement] is a joining-together of two parts, the first as ante-
18 cedent | and the other as consequent.

The minor[4] of the two premisses [of a conditional syllogism] is a categorical [statement]. It is this statement to which the "exclusive" particle is connected[5] [in the major pre-
19 miss], | for it is itself one of the two parts of the major
20 premiss in a conditional syllogism. | It [i.e., the minor premiss] is called "the excluded". Sometimes the antecedent and sometimes the consequent is "excluded", except that
258 the first syllogism || among the condition syllogisms[6] [is such that] in it only the antecedent itself is "excluded", and then it yields the consequent itself.[7]

---

[3] Note this technical use of the root *q-r-n* ("to connect").
[4] I suppose *ṣ-gh-r-y* for the *d-r-w-r-y* of M. Türker's text.
[5] Again the comment of footnote 3 applies.
[6] Viz., the conjunctive conditional syllogism.
[7] "Exclusion" in the present sense has nothing to do with negation. A statement is "excluded" when it appears in the premisses but not

2 | The conditional [premiss of a syllogism] can be composed not only of two affirmatives alone, but also of two
3 negatives, as in the statement | "If the sun has not risen, it is not day"; or of an affirmative and a negative, as in
4 the statement "If it is not night-time, | it is daytime". [Furthermore] the antecedent can be a plurality of state-
5 ments [i.e., a conjunction], as in the statement, | "If a (corporeal) body is not fixed in place, and it is in motion,
6 and its motion is a linear motion, | and a linear motion is only [possible] towards a distance at a greater measure of
7 remoteness from the moving object, | and the distant is very remote, and the remote is different from that which is only a little separated, then a [linearly moving] body must go
8 to some place wholly other [than its initial place]". | Now the antecedent in this conditional is a plurality of statements, and the consequent is a single statement.

(b) Negative Mode (Modus Tollens)

9 | Now as for the second [kind of] conjunctive conditional [syllogism], it is as follows: "If the cause is not a single
10 one, | then the world is not an orderly system; but the world is an orderly system; it follows that the cause is single".[8]
11 This syllogism does not | differ from [the pattern of] the first [kind] in its major [i.e., conditional] premiss, but only differs from it in its "excluded" [i.e., minor] premiss. When
12 | in a conjunctive conditional [syllogism] the antecedent "part" itself is "excluded", the first [kind of] conditional
13 [syllogism] arises; and if | the opposite of the consequent

---

in the conclusion. To "exclude" a statement in manner al-Fārābī has in view invariably involves its *assertion*! The Arabic word in question, *istathnā'*, corresponds to Greek *proslēpsis*, for which see Kneale, *The Development of Logic*, pp. 106–109, and 163.

[8] This second kind of conjunctive conditional syllogism (viz., its negative mode):

If P then Q
Not Q
∴ Not P

This is the *modus tollens* of the Latin logicians.

is "excluded", the second [kind of conjunctive] conditional [syllogism] results, and it yields the opposite of the antecedent.

14 The consequent | in this second [kind of conjunctive conditional] syllogism must be a statement that is denied (negated). For example: "If unlimited corporeal substance
15 | is in existence, then it is either simple or compound; but
16 unlimited corporeal substance is neither simple nor | compound; and so unlimited corporeal substance is not in existence".

258   (ii) DISJUNCTIVE CONDITIONAL SYLLOGISMS

17 | The second [kind of] conditional syllogisms is called a
18 *disjunctive* conditional. This can have | many forms. For example: "Either the world is eternal or it is originated, but the world is originated, so it necessarily results that the
19 world is not | eternal".[9] The conditional of these two [premisses] is the statement beginning with "either", which
20 presents the alternative | of one of two items to the other, and opposes it to, and disjoins it from the other.

Now the antecedent of the two "parts" of the conditional
21 premiss | is that one of the two which meets these two conditions, [namely] that it comes first in the [conditional] statement, and it is whichever of the two precedes its neigh-
259 bor.[10] Thus consider the statement, "The world || is either originated or it is eternal". The antecedent is the statement, "The world is originated". And if we had put the
2 other [statement] first, then it would have been | the antecedent.

The two "parts" of a conditional here are always two

[9] The simple disjunctive conditional syllogism thus takes the form:

$$\frac{P \text{ or } Q \text{ (but not both)}}{Q}$$
$$\therefore \text{Not } P$$

This is *modus ponendo tollens* of the (exclusive) disjunctive syllogism of the Latin logicians.

[10] I suppose *j-'-r* for the *j-'-z* of M. Türker's text.

[mutually incompatible] alternatives. And likewise when there are | more than two "parts" to this [premiss] they will also be mutually opposed. And the alternatives which are stipulated | are either only two—as with the statement, "The world is either eternal or originated"—or | more than two—as with the statement, "Zaid is either white or black or red".

Every [disjunctive statement] is of | one of the following two types: either it is a complete (i.e., exhaustive) alternative or it is an incomplete (i.e., non-exhaustive) alternative. A *complete* [i.e., exhaustive] alternative is one that includes within itself | all the [possible] alternatives whatsoever, be they two or more; like the statement "The world is either eternal or originated", or the statement, | "This water is either hot or cold or lukewarm". But an *imperfect* [i.e., non-exhaustive] alternative is one that does not include within itself | all of the alternatives, like the statement "Zaid is either in Iraq or in Syria", and [the statement] "Zaid is either white | or black or red".

Every disjunctive conditional [syllogism] whose alternatives are two only, and | whose alternatives are complete, [is such that] when either one of them [viz., the two alternatives] is "excluded", the conclusion agrees with the opposite of the other alternative; and if the opposite of either one of them is "excluded", | then this yields the other alternative itself. An example of this is: "The number is either even or it is odd". Because it [i.e., a number] is either | even, and consequently it is not odd, or it is odd, and consequently not even; or it is not even, and consequently odd, | or it is not odd, and consequently even.

When there are more than two [alternatives] and the alternative is | complete, then if one of them is "excluded", this yields the opposite of the rest. Such is the statement: "This | number is either greater than or less than or equal to [some given number], but this number is equal, and therefore it is neither greater nor less". If | one "excludes" the opposite of two of them [i.e., of the three alternatives],

this yields the remaining one, as in the example: "This
number is either greater or | less or equal, so if it [i.e.,
the number] is neither less nor greater, then it must consequently be equal". This circumstance will also obtain
when the alternatives [of a disjunctive statement] are | more
than three, *mutatis mutandis*. And if one "excludes" the
opposite of one of them, this yields | the remainder [of the
alternatives], as it is supposed to do. Thus when [the statement] "This number is not the equal" is "excluded", this
yields that, "It [i.e., this number] is | either greater or less".
And then whatever [statement] "excludes" the opposite of
one of the remaining [alternatives], will yield the [other]
remaining [alternatively]. When || it is supposed that
[only] two alternatives remain, then if one "excludes" the
opposite of one of them, this yields | the factuality of the
other.[11]

If the alternative is imperfect, then if one of the two
[alternatives] is "excluded", then [the conclusion] necessarily agrees with the opposite of the other [alternative].
| [On the other hand] if one "excludes" the opposite one of
[viz., one of the two imperfect alternatives, say the antecedent one], there does not necessarily follow anything
whatever, neither the consequent [itself], nor the opposite
of the consequent. | An example is [the argument]: "Zaid
is either in Iraq or Syria or the Hijaz, but he is in Iraq,
so he consequently is neither | in Syria nor in the Hijaz".
But if it is "excluded" that he is not in Iraq, then it does

---

[11] Thus we have, on the one hand, the arguments,

| P or Q (but not both) | P or Q (but not both) |
P	Q
Not Q	Not P

and on the other hand, since the alternatives are complete, we also have:

| P or Q (but not both) | P or Q (but not both) |
Not P	Not Q
Q	P

6 not necessarily follow that he is in Syria | or [that he is] in the Hijaz. [It does not follow] that he is not in one or the other of them except when it has been shown or sup-
7 posed that he will not vacate the domain | of one of them, and that he has not already vacated its realm; for then the character [of the imperfect alternative] is [akin to] the
8 character of a complete [alternative]. | [Given] the major premiss of a [disjunctive] conditional [syllogism] which has imperfect alternatives—[like "Zaid is in Iraq or Syria or
9 the Hijaz"]—it would be best to say: | "Zaid is not in Iraq, but he is either in Syria or in the Hijaz"; then it is [explicitly] "excluded" that he is [not!] in Iraq.
10 | These are the conditional syllogisms. Their kinds remain [to be considered]. We shall return to that.[12]

[12] This promise is not kept within the confines of the present treatise.

Section 5

"OBJECTING" SYLLOGISMS

| Let us now speak about "objecting" syllogisms.
| If an assertoric syllogism is such that both its premisses are evidently true then it is called | a *sound* syllogism, and it yields a conclusion that is inescapably true.[1] For example: "All corporeal substance (C) is composite (K), and all | K is created (R); so consequently, all C is R".

If one of the two premisses [of a valid syllogism] | is clearly in accordance with the truth, and the other is doubtful, it not being known whether it is | true or false, and the conclusion is evidently false, then this syllogism is called an "*objecting*" syllogism.[2] | There is shown by this the truth of the opposite of the doubtful one of the two premisses of the syllogism. | This [opposite] is to be made the conclusion of the syllogism.

For example: "The world is eternal, but no single eternal thing is composite, so it follows that the world | is not composite". This [conclusion] is clearly false, and yet is contained, as a consequence, in the syllogism. However, | one of its premisses is clearly true, namely "No single eternal thing is composite". Falsity | thus can only reach

---

[1] The following possibilities arise with respect to valid syllogisms.

The premisses are	The conclusion is
(1) both true	true (by necessity)
(2a) ⎰ one true, one false	true
(2b) ⎱ one true, one false	false
(3a) ⎰ both false	true
(3b) ⎱ both false	false

In case (1) al-Fārābī calls the syllogism *sound* (*mustaqīm*).

[2] An "objecting" syllogism exists when the conclusion is known to be false and one premiss known to be true. We must thus be in case (2b) above, and the falsity of the remaining premiss is assured. The ultimate (but indeed remote) basis for the idea of "objecting" syllogisms is *Anal. Pr.* II, 26.

the conclusion from the other premiss—that which it effects
is false, and so it is false [itself]. || In consequence the statement "The world is eternal" is false, and thus its contradictory is consequently true, namely the statement "The world is not eternal". | This then is the conclusion which follows from the "objecting" syllogism.

When we wish to conclude something by means of an "objecting" syllogism, | then we must suppose [the denial of] what we wish to conclude. Thus, if this [desired conclusion] is the sentence "The world is not eternal", | we take its contradictory, namely "The world is eternal", and add to it another premiss which is clearly true, | and is such that when it is added the union of the two becomes a syllogism, namely "No single eternal thing | is composite". Then [the two together] yield as conclusion "The world is not composite". But we find that this conclusion is evidently false. Therefore it is necessitated | by this that "The world is not eternal".[3]

| This completes the totality of [all of the kinds of] simple syllogisms.[4]

---

[3] The logical character of the "objecting" syllogism is as follows: We wish to establish a conclusion C. We find a valid syllogism whose conclusion C* is false, and whose premisses consist of the *negation* of C and some other true premiss P. Thus,

$$\frac{P \quad \text{not-}C}{C^*}$$

is a valid syllogism, and so, therefore, is (what we would call its "antilogism"):

$$\frac{P \quad \text{not-}C^*}{C}$$

But P is true (*ex hypothesi*) and not-C* is true (since C* is false, *ex hypothesi*), so that—in view of the validity of the syllogism—C is true. Q.E.D.

[4] The "simple" syllogism would thus be the categorical, the conditional, and the "objecting" syllogisms. These stand in contrast to the "compound" syllogisms to be dealt with in the next section.

Section 6

COMPOUND SYLLOGISMS

261   (i) TRANSITION

8   Let us now speak about the compound syllogism. The
9 | syllogisms we have enumerated [above] are not always used
10 only in the compositions we have discussed. Nor are | the premisses[1] and conclusions of all syllogisms expressed with full accuracy, without being misleading in any respect.
11 Rather, | their composition is changed frequently, and many of their premisses[2] are omitted, while other things are added,
12 | which may not [actually] be a support for drawing the conclusion. [Indeed] this is the customary practice in
13 discourses and in | books.

261   (ii) DIGRESSION ON TRANSFORMING NON-
            SYLLOGISMS INTO SYLLOGISMS

Whenever a statement [i.e., an argument] is not composed in one of the modes of composition[3] which we have discussed
14 [above], then there is an increase in it or | a decrease, and its order has been changed. Then [if] its composition becomes one of the compositions we have discussed, and
15 yet the meaning | of the original statement remains in the same state it was before the change, then the original statement was a syllogism.
16   And whenever a statement is such that, [when] | one of the compositions we have discussed is substituted in its place, the meaning is changed from that of the original
17 statement—so that the meaning of the second | becomes changed from the meaning of the original—then the original is not syllogistic, and it is not at all feasible that [these

---

[1] Literally: *parts*. In this section this substitution is frequent.
[2] Literally: *parts*.
[3] Literally: *in one of the compositions*.

18 statements] should be the two premises | of a syllogism which is composed of two knowns, in one of the "four ways".⁴

261 (iii) COMPOUND SYLLOGISMS (RESUMED)

19 [A syllogism] may be composed of two premises | both of which, or one of which are [themselves] known through a syllogism, [so that] it may not be feasible, in this syllogism,
20 | that one or both of the two premises are known from the outset.⁵ But frequently it is necessary for one or both
262 || [of the premises of a syllogism] to be established by a syllogism also. Then it continues on in this way until it
2 ends in a syllogism | composed of two premises which are known from the outset in one of the "four ways".⁶
3 | Thus, if we wish to show something by a syllogism, then the premises must also be known through a syllogism.
4 Then | the premisses of this syllogism need to be established
5 by syllogisms, until this [process] finally terminates | in syllogisms whose premises are known from the outset. The
6 method here is to show this | by syllogisms whose premises are known from the outset, and then either, (1) to take the
7 conclusions and add them | to other premises, or (2) to add them all together and then to take the conclusions of
8 these and add them to | other premises, or (3) to add them all together until this ends in two premises [of such a sort
9 that] if | we compose them, we obtain a syllogism which yields from the two [premises] the conclusion which was sought-for from the outset.⁷

⁴ I have labeled this discussion a *digression* to call attention to its being somewhat loose from the moorings of its context.

⁵ Or: *from the beginning*. I am tempted to use *a priori*, but want to avoid Kantian associations. The point is that such premises need not be of some special kind, but simply that they be conceded as known. Cf. 249: 20 and following.

⁶ This paragraph indicates the rationale in which "compound syllogisms" arise—namely when the premises of a given syllogism themselves require syllogistic demonstration so that we are driven to a chain of syllogisms (going back to ultimate premises that are "known from the outset") which lead to the conclusion in question.

⁷ The "compound syllogism" then pre-eminently includes *en-*

10 | But if we make fully explicit all the parts [i.e., premisses] of these syllogisms, we draw the statement out to great
11 length. | Therefore, we limit ourselves in many cases of such premisses to a part of them [only], and omit certain of them
12 which are already contained in | what has been made explicit, or [in what] is plain [and] obvious or [in what] speech itself necessitates.
13 | For example, when it is said that someone is an oathbreaker, then it is known that he is a man-who-has-sworn. Another example, if it is said that the money has been
14 weighed then it is known | that it has been balanced-on-a-scale.

Thus a syllogism can be a compound of many syllogisms,
15 some of whose premisses[8] are omitted, | and [what is explicitly given] being limited to some of them, as though the explicitly given premisses[9] were the whole.
16 If we wish, for example, to show that | "The world is created", by means of the following syllogism, "Every corporeal substance is composite, and every composite thing
17 is 'contingent', | so it follows that every corporeal substance
18 is 'contingent' ", then we take this conclusion, | and we add to it, "Everything 'contingent' is inseparably united to a
19 creator". | From this it follows that "Every corporeal substance is inseparably united to a creator". Now we take
20 this | conclusion and we add to it, "Everything inseparably
21 united to a creator is not prior to its creator". | Thereupon it follows that, "Every corporeal substance is not prior to its creator". Now we take the conclusion of this third
263 syllogism || and add to it, "Everything not prior to its creator will then come into being with the existence of the
2 creator". Thereupon it follows | that, "Every corporeal substance comes into being with the existence of its creator".

---

thymemes and *sorites*. Aristotle adverts to the "prosyllogisms" only very passingly in *Anal. Pr.* (42b5, 66a35). But for enthymemes, see II, 27.

[8] Literally: *parts.*   [9] Literally: *parts.*

3 Then we take this conclusion, and we add to it, | "Everything that comes into being with the existence of its creator, comes into being in time". Thereupon it follows that,
4 "Every | corporeal substance comes into being in time". Then we add to the conclusion of this fifth syllogism
5 "Everything that | comes into being in time is created in existence".[10] Thereupon it follows that, "Every corporeal
6 substance is created in existence". | Then we add to the conclusion of this sixth syllogism that, "The world is a
7 corporeal substance". Thereupon it follows by | a seventh syllogism that, "The world is created".

However, if all of the premises[11] of this [argument] are
8 given, the statement is drawn out to great length. | Thus it is necessary that we omit those premises of these syllogisms which are conclusions of preceding syllogisms,
9 | and limit ourselves to those which are not conclusions, since those [statements] which are conclusions are already
10 contained | in those which yield them [as conclusions]. Then we come finally, after all this, to the ultimate conclusion.

For example, consider again the argument: "Every cor-
11 poreal substance | is composite, and everything composite is
12 'contingent', and everything 'contingent' | is inseparately united to a creator, and everything inseparately united to
13 a creator does not | precede its creator, and everything that does not precede its creator comes into existence with the
14 existence of its creator, and everything that | comes into being with the existence of its creator comes into being in
15 time, and everything that comes into being in time | is created, and the world is a corporeal substance, so it follows that the world is created". This example is a compound syllogism.
16 | The compounds [i.e., compound syllogisms] may be [composed] of syllogisms of different kinds. For example,
17 they may include some conditional [syllogisms] | and some assertoric [syllogisms], and some "objecting" syllogisms,

[10] Literally: *exists after its non-existence.* [11] Literally: *parts.*

and some sound syllogisms.¹² And they may be [composed] of sound syllogisms | of various different figures.

For example: "The world is inescapably either eternal | or created; now if it is eternal then it is not 'contingent'; but it is 'contingent', || because it is corporeal; now the corporeal, if not 'contingent' must be devoid of it [i.e., contingency]; but what is devoid | of it is not composite, and it is impossible to move it from¹³ that state; so it follows that the world is created". This | syllogism is compounded of a disjunctive conditional and a conjunctive conditional, and there is [also] an assertoric [syllogism] by the method | of "objection" and a sound assertoric [syllogism].¹⁴

¹² The formulation is somewhat careless, since both sound and "opposing" syllogisms are special cases of categorical syllogisms, differentiated by the truth-states of their premisses. See 260: 12-13 above.

¹³ I suppose 'an for the wa of M. Türker's text.

¹⁴ At this point, the discussion of "syllogisms" as such is completed. The remainder of the treatise is concerned to show how various other modes of inference (e.g., induction, analogy, "example") reduce, insofar as valid, to syllogistic inference.

Section 7

INDUCTION

264

5, 6   Let us now speak about induction. | *Induction* is the "investigation" of things included within some "matter",
7 in order to show the truth of some judgment | about this "matter", by denial or affirmation.

Now if we wish to affirm or to deny a "thing" of a
8 "matter", then we must "investigate" | the things which are embraced by this "matter". And [if] we find this
9 "thing" in all of them, or in most of them, | then we show thereby that the "thing" is to be found in this "matter". Or, [if] we "investigate" them [i.e., the things embraced by the "matter"], and do not find this "thing", not even
10 | in a single one of them, then we show thereby that this "thing" does not exist in this "matter". This "investiga-
11 tion" is | induction. Thus the conclusion of an induction is the affirmation[1] of or denial to the "matter" of this "thing" [which has been "investigated"].

12   For example, | if we wish to show that "Every motion takes place in time", we must "investigate" the [various]
13 species of motion, namely | walking, flying, swimming, and the like. Then [when] we find that every one of them takes
14 place in time, [the conclusion] is reached | that "Every motion takes place in time".

Induction is an argument[2] that has the force of a syllo-
15 gism in the first figure. | The middle term in it [i.e., induction] is the things which are investigated, namely [in the
16 example] walking and flying and swimming. | And the major[3] [term] is the expression "within time". Thus [the syllogism] is composed as follows: "Every motion is walking

---

[1] I suppose '-*th-b-*'-*t* for the '-*y-j-*'-*b* of M. Türker's text.
[2] Literally: *a statement.*
[3] I suppose '-*k-b-r* for the '-*k-th-r* of M. Türker's text.

Al-Fārābī's Short Commentary 89

17 or flying or | swimming and other things of that kind; but walking and flying and the rest [all] take place in time;
18 | so it follows that every motion takes place in time".[4]
19 Similarly, if someone wished to show that "Every | agent is corporeal", and he "investigated" the species of agents, such as the builder and the tailor and the shoemaker and the
20 like, | then [if] he found that every one of these is corporeal, he judges in consequence that "Every agent is corporeal".
21 | He has shown this by an induction. It is composed as
265 follows: "Every agent is a builder, || or a tailor, or a shoemaker, or some other type of agent; and every builder or
2 tailor, etc., is corporeal; | so it follows that every agent is corporeal".[5]

It is known that it is not possible to judge [with certainty]
3 after an "investigation" that "Every agent | is corporeal", unless one has investigated *all* the kinds of agents, until not a single one of them has been left out. For if a single one
4 of them remains | uninvestigated, or [even after investigation] one of them is such that it is not known whether it is corporeal or not, then it is not possible to judge about
5 every | agent [whatsoever] that it is corporeal.

[4] The pattern of an induction is thus as follows:

Known major:	All members of the group G are Z's
Inductive minor—substitutes "Most X's are G's" for:	All X's are members of the group G
Desired conclusion:	All X's are Z's

In the example we thus have the Barbara syllogism:
Major: All members of the group (walking, flying, swimming . . .) are temporal
Minor: Most [for "All"] motions are members of the group (walking, flying, swimming . . .)
Conclusion: All motions are temporal

[5] This example again fits the above pattern:
Major: All members of the group (builder, tailor, shoemaker, . . .) are corporeal
Minor: Most [for "All"] agents are members of the group (builder, tailor, shoemaker, . . .)
Conclusion: All agents are corporeal

6 | Induction is sometimes *complete* and sometimes *incomplete*. Complete [induction] occurs when one "investigates"
7 *all* the kinds | of things included within the subject of the premiss which one intends to establish by the induction. And
8 defective [i.e., incomplete] [induction] | consists in "investigating" *most* [though not all] of the kinds of these things.

What is shown by an induction may be intended to be
9 shown solely with the limited purpose | of knowing it, and this alone. Or it may be intended to be shown in order to be used as a premiss in a syllogism which is intended [in
10 turn] to show | some other thing about the subject whose contents we "investigated" [in the induction]. For example,
11 if we wish to show that "Every | motion takes place in time", we "investigate" the kinds of motion, in order to add
12 to it that "Everything that takes place in time | is created", to conclude from this that "Every motion is created". Thus
13 induction can be very useful | in showing something to be the case, if it is employed in a syllogism. It is employed in this way, that [to continue with the foregoing example] we
14 make that which is shown by the induction | to exist in motion—namely *being in time*—the middle term [of a syllo-
15 gism] that shows the existence | of some other thing in motion, as for example that "Every motion is created".[6]

It may be intended to show something by an induction
16 | in order to use this thing as [universal] premiss in a syllogism which is [in turn] intended to prove that the predicate
17 of the premiss belongs to something else | that is included within its subject.[7] For example, [it may be intended] to

---

[6] The syllogism in question is the AAA-1 (Barbara) syllogism of the preceding paragraph, as follows:

> All that takes place in time is created
> All motion takes place in time
> ---
> All motion is created

The inductive premiss here is the minor: "All motion takes place in time".

[7] The line of reasoning sketched in this paragraph is criticized in the ensuing discussion.

show by induction that "Every motion takes place in time", in order to use this | to show that swimming, for instance, takes place in time. Then the syllogism would be composed as follows: "Every motion takes place in time, | and swimming is a motion, so it follows that it [viz., swimming] takes place in time".[8]

Induction, in this case, is used to show that "Every motion takes place in | time", in order to establish as true by this that some species of motion, like swimming or anything else similar to it | that is included within [the genus] motion [takes place in time]. [But this procedure is questionable.] For this species [of motion] is not left out of what must be "investigated" if one intends | to show [by an induction] that "Every motion takes place in time". [But swimming itself is either "investigated"] or it is not "investigated".

(1) But if it *is not* "investigated"—or it is [actually] "investigated", but it is [nevertheless] not known whether | it takes place in time or not—so that swimming remains of unknown status as regards motion—then it is not possible for us to conclude || that "Every motion takes place in time". And if we do not know that "Every motion takes place in time", then it is not possible | we should know [by the syllogism here in question] that swimming, being a motion, takes place in time or not, [for then] swimming is [possibly] | not contained within that part of the motions which take place in time.

(2) If it [i.e., swimming] *is* "investigated", and it is known | that it takes place in time, then it is evident that we made this "investigation" prior to knowing that "Every motion takes place in time". Thus there is not | after that any

---

[8] That is, the intended argument may have the pattern:

Inductive (major) premiss:	Most [for "All"] Y's are Z's
Known minor:	All X's are Y's
Conclusion:	All X's are Z's

Here then it is the *major* premiss, rather than the *minor* as above, that is arrived at through induction.

need for us to show [by some syllogism] that swimming takes place in time. If we sought to show this | it would be evident that we are only seeking to show a thing through a "matter" which is [itself] shown by means of that thing. And we also seek | to show a thing which is more known to us through that which is less known.[9]

Thus it has been shown that induction cannot | serve to show the truth of a thing to be used as a [universal] premiss in a syllogism which is intended to prove its predicate to belong to something | included within its subject, or [for that matter] to disprove it. For this reason, it is not possible to show that God, the All-powerful and the All-great | is corporeal by the argument, "God is an agent, and every agent is corporeal", when the statement "Every agent | is corporeal" is only shown by an induction over the [various] kinds of agents.

Thus it has been shown how induction goes back to [i.e., reduces to] the syllogism, and where | it is serviceable, and where not.[10]

[9] Al-Fārābī's dilemma can be outlined as follows, using the pattern of footnote 8 above:
  (1) By the minor premiss we know that the X's are Y's.
  (2) When the induction-survey of the Y's is made to establish the major premiss that the Y's are Z's, the X's are either investigated or they are not.
  (3) If they *are not* investigated then we have not completed the job of establishing the induction premiss to the effect that *all* the Y's are Z's.
  (4) But if they *are* investigated then we have a direct finding, and the syllogistic argument is either erroneous or superfluous.

[10] The short section on induction in *Anal. Pr.* II, 23 (68b8–38; and compare *Topica* I, 12) does not contain anything that could be regarded as the basis of al-Fārābī's analysis of the conditions under which induction is (or is not) a legitimate means to a syllogistic premiss. His treatment of induction is more systematic and detailed than that of *Anal. Pr.*

Section 8

INFERENCE BY "TRANSFER"
(i.e., ANALOGY)

8-1. THE METHOD OF "TRANSFER"

(i) INTRODUCTORY CONSIDERATIONS

| It is now necessary that we discuss the "transfer" from a judgment by [immediate] sensation in some matter, or [direct] knowledge about it | by some other approach, to another matter outside the realm of [immediate] sensation. A judgment stems from another [source than sensation], when this other [unsensed] matter | is subordinated to the first [i.e., sensed] matter. This is what the people of our time[1] call "inference from evidence to the absent". | The manner of this "transfer" is: that it is known by sensation that a certain "matter" is in a certain condition, and that a certain "thing" | is present in a certain "matter"; and so the intellect consequently transfers this condition or thing from this [known] matter to some other [unknown] matter | similar to it, and thus judges with respect to it [i.e., the other, unknown, "matter"] upon this [known] basis.[2] This occurs [for example] when one knows by sensation

---
[1] The "people of our time", to whose views al-Fārābī is by and large opposed, are presumably the philosophical theologians (*mutakallimūn*).

[2] The terminology and the character of inference by "transfer" is thus as follows. There are two "matters" A and B, which exhibit a point of similarity S. (On the importance of the similarity for such reasoning, see *Topica*, 108b10–14.) It is known that in one of these "matters", say A, a certain "thing" T is present. The reasoning is then as follows:

Since A and B are both similar in respect of S, and since T is present in A, we may conclude that T is present in B.

This clearly answers to the argument by analogy. "Transfer" is Aristotle's *apagogē*, for which see *Anal. Pr.* II, 25.

that some corporeal substances,[3] like the animals and similar
things, | are created, and consequently the intellect transfers
the createdness from the animals or plants, and thus judges
about the sky and the stars | that they are [also] created.
But it is only possible that one can "transfer" [createdness]
from the animals to the sky, and thus to impute to it [viz.,
the sky] the createdness which | was found by sensation[4] in
the animals, if the animals and the sky exhibit a similarity;
and not just any agreeing similarity at all, || but a similarity
in some matter that is *relevant* to the characterization of the
animals as created.[5] That is, there must be a similarity
| between the animals and the sky in a matter which lends
truth to the judgment that createdness pertains to this
entire matter, such as "being contingent",[6] | for example.
For if it is known by sensation that the animals are created
and that they are similar to the sky in respect of being
"contingent", | and [if] the judgment regarding createdness
is true about everything that is "contingent", then the
"transfer" | of createdness from the animals to the sky will
be a true one. But if the judgment that it is created is not
[assumed as] true of everything "contingent", | and the sky
is "contingent", then it is not possible [to make] the "trans-
fer" [of createdness] from the animals to the sky, | before
[it has been shown that] it is possible that createdness
actually exists in everything "contingent". [The "transfer"]
is bound to the condition which draws [the conclusion about]
the sky | from a similarity with the animals in a matter

---

[3] Literally: *bodies*.   [4] Literally: *sensed*.

[5] The general discussion, as well as the example, indicate that the process of "inference by transfer" takes the form:

Premiss 1: All X's are Y's
Premiss 2: The Z's resemble the X's in a respect that is *relevant* to their being Y's
_____
Conclusion: All Z's are (also) Y's

The immediately following discussion addresses itself to establishing the need for the relevancy clause of the second premiss.

[6] Literally: *being connected with contingent creations*.

relating to the createdness of the animals; because created-
ness is only found | as something actually present in animals
due to a connection with "being contingent", through some
special form of connection. This form of connection is not
to be found | in [the case of] the sky. Therefore, when the
situation is of this kind, then it is not possible at all for the
"transfer" to be maintained.

| When it has not actually been shown that everything
"contingent" is created, but we have only obtained by | a
"transferral" [the conclusion] that the "contingent" is
created, then one who makes the "transfer", transfers from
the judgment regarding the animals to [that regarding] | the
sky. He has thus made a "transfer" to that which is possibly
similar to the animals, not [really] in regard to the "thing"
which is responsible | for the finding of "contingency" in
them. Then the "transfer" is not actually correct, but it
is only imagined that it is an evident inference, | [and] is
correct.

If we are determined to have the "transfer" be correct,
then it is necessary that the "matter" which | is similar in
the two [compared] objects be investigated. The judgment
regarding the createdness of the totality is correct when
everything "contingent" is | created. [For then] if the sky
is similar to the animals in being "contingent", then it
necessarily follows that | the sky is created. The force of
this [inference] becomes [the same as] the force of the
arrangement of the syllogism in the first figure, namely:
| "The sky is 'contingent', and everything 'contingent' is
created, therefore it follows that the sky is created".[7]

---

[7] The point is that the "transfer" is a strictly valid inference only when the relevancy condition (Premiss 2 of the preceding footnote) takes the maximally strong form of "All Z's are X's", so that we have AAA-1 (Barbara) syllogism. Al-Fārābī's response to the "people of our time" who endorse the "inference by a 'transfer' from evidence towards the absent" is to put before them the dilemma: When the "transfer" is valid, a syllogistic inference will do the job; when a syllogism won't serve, the "transfer" is an invalid inference.

267 (ii) THE METHODS OF ANALYSIS AND
OF SYNTHESIS

20 | The "(inference by) transfer from evidence to the absent" is of two sorts: (1) by the method of synthesis,
21 | and (2) by the method of analysis. The analysis [procedure] occurs when "the absent" is taken as the basic point of
22 departure. | The synthesis [procedure] occurs when the [actually available] evidence is taken as the basic point of departure.

268 If we wish to draw a conclusion || about "the absent" from the evidence by the method of analysis, then it is necessary that we know the judgment which is sought for
2 | regarding "the absent". Then we investigate in which of the sensory facts one can "find" this judgment [to obtain]. Then once we know the sensory fact which is embodied in
3 | this judgment, we will take up one of those "matters" in which a similarity exists between [the sought-for judgment regarding] "the absent" and this sensory fact. Then we find
4 out in which | one of those various "matters" the judgment which gives evidence about the sensory facts is [also] true in its entirety [i.e., also with respect to "the absent"]. Then
5 if | we "find" such a matter, then there is a "transfer" by necessity of the judgment from the sensory evidence to
6 the absent. | Consequently, "the inference from evidence to the absent" has by this method the power to provide
7 the sought-for answer. And | the syllogism which leads to its conclusion is to be found in the first figure.[8]

[8] The terminology and the reasoning of "transfer by the method of analysis" is as follows. Let:
  (a) A be "the absent" matter.
  (b) "All A's are X's" be "the judgment" which is sought for regarding A.
  (c) P be "the present" sensory fact in which the judgment can be "found", so that "All P's are X's".
  (d) S be "the similarity" between A and P, so that both "All A's are S's" and "All P's are S's".
The reasoning is now as follows:
Since the A's, which are S's, are also X's, we suppose that "All S's are

8 | If we wish to have an "inference from evidence to the absent" which [proceeds] by the method of synthesis, we
9   must [first] investigate | some sensory fact which provides evidence for a certain judgment. We then take the other matters which are actually present in this [given]
10 sensory fact. | Then we investigate in which one of those various matters that judgment is [also] true in its entirety.
11 And so, if we obtain this | then we have "found" something outside our knowledge, a judgment which is applicable
12 under this matter. It follows by necessity that | there is a "transfer" to it [i.e., "the absent"] of the judgment which was known by us to be true as a sensory fact. The manner
13 of this [inference] is also of the force | of a syllogism of the first figure.[9]

Now the "matter" which is present in the whole [of the inference, i.e., the similarity "found" in both "the absent" and "the present" sensory fact] is called by the people of

---

X's". Now this together with "All A's are S's" yields the syllogism:

    All S's are X's
    All A's are S's
    ∴ All A's are X's

As al-Fārābī observes, the inference is thus achieved by a first-figure syllogism, in which the similarity S serves as the middle term.

[9] The terminology and the reasoning of "transfer by the method of synthesis" is as follows. Let:
(a) P be "the present" sensory fact.
(b) "All P's are X's" be the judgment which is "found" about P.
(c) S be "the similarity" between P and "the absent" matter, A, so that "All P's are S's" and "All A's are S's".

The reasoning is now as follows:
Since the P's, which are S's, are also X's, we suppose that "All S's are X's". Now this together with "All A's are S's" yields the syllogism:

    All S's are X's
    All A's are S's
    All A's are X's

This syllogism, identical with that of the preceding footnote, is, as al-Fārābī observes, a first-figure syllogism, with the similarity S serving as the middle term.

14 our time[10] | "the cause"; and it is [in actuality] the middle term [of the syllogism].[11, 11a]
15 | The correctness of a judgment about some particular "matter" in which the "absent" resembles the [actually
16 available] evidence may be known to us in many | cases by itself, without any syllogism or thinking or contemplation at all, in the same [immediate] way in which a "first pre-
17 miss" is known | in one of the "four ways".[11b] That whose correctness is not known by itself [i.e., is not self-evident]
18 requires | some other thing for its establishment. This may be done in any one of these modes [of syllogism], so that
19 it is shown to be true by a syllogism composed | in any one of the ways we have discussed above, either categorical or conditional.

8-2. THE METHOD OF "INVESTIGATION"

(i) DIRECT EMPLOYMENT

20 We may also "investigate" the species | of the "matter". If we "find" some judgment that holds for everything [i.e., every species] falling under it [i.e., the "matter"], then this judgment will be true about the whole of this "matter".[12]

---

[10] Cf. 266: 15 above.

[11] Note that in this paragraph, and that preceding, the point is again urged that inference by "transfer" amounts, when valid, to syllogistic inference.

[11a] It would be of interest to have further information regarding this concept of "cause". Cf. also 273: 11 below.

[11b] The text reads: *three*.

[12] The situation here is as follows. Let:

M, the "matter" have the species $S_1, S_2, \ldots$, so that "All M's are $(S_1$'s or S_2's or $\ldots)$".

Now suppose that some (correct) judgment "finds" a thing X to be present in each of these species. We then obtain the syllogism:

$$\frac{\text{All } (S_1\text{'s or } S_2\text{'s or } \ldots) \text{ are X's}}{\text{All M's are } (S_1\text{'s or } S_2\text{'s or } \ldots)}$$
$$\therefore \text{ All M's are X's}$$

This is a first-figure syllogism, with the family of species that are "investigated" (S_1's or S_2's, etc.), serving as the middle term.

21 | And if it [the judgment] is not "found" in any of them [i.e., the species], then it must be true that it is not to be found
22 in any of that "matter". And if | it is clear in some of its species only that the judgment is not true about it [viz., the entire "matter"], then it is false that it obtains about all of it.[13] It is [thus] false that it [i.e., the judgment] holds
269 for || the whole ["matter"], and the premiss [of the syllogism representing the argument] becomes particular [so that a syllogism with a universal conclusion is impossible].

Thus something is shown to be true by this [species-
2 directed] method, only when it is shown to be true | by the "transfer" of a judgment which is true about the whole of this "matter", to some part of what falls under it. This
3 method is | useless in "inference from evidence to the
4 absent", because if that to which | we made the transfer were something open to "investigation", then we would "find" this judgment [itself], and so would already know this
5 judgment | itself, without making any "transfer" to it, and before we knew of the existence of the "matter" in regard
6 to which | the absent resembles the sensory [evidence]. Therefore we have no need to make any "transfer" to it [viz., the judgment]. But if it were not open to "investiga-
7 tion", | or [if it were] open to "investigation", but not unknown, whether this judgment is to be predicated of it or not, [then] it could not be known that the judgment is true
8 about the whole of this | matter. But then, if that is not true, the "transfer to the absent" is not true [either], in accordance with what was said in [the section on] induc-
9 tion.[14] For it has already | been demonstrated that it is not possible to show to be true by this method the factuality of a judgment on the basis of the whole of some "matter" which pertains [only] to the cause.

269 (ii) ARGUMENTS OF REFUTATION

10 | As to [the case] when the judgment is assumed to be

[13] That is, the affirmative universal judgment will not be true.
[14] See 265: 15–266: 7.

factual with respect to all of that "matter" [in question], it is possible by this method to refute a universal judgment.
11 | Now this method is what the people of our time[15] call
12 "to derive a judgment about a cause from | the effects". They mean by the "effects" those things which are derived from the "matter" which is supposed as the cause. The
13 judgment | which the cause renders necessary[16] is [either] that whose truth is sought-for in the whole of that "matter",
14 or else is that which is assumed | as factual for the whole of it. The pursuit of that judgment, or its parts, about the
15 causes consists in the "investigation" of | each one of the things which fall under the "matter" assumed as the cause.
16   It has been demonstrated that | the pursuit which can render necessary a cause by a "judgment from the effects"
17 is not of any use for rendering true a judgment | about the supposed cause, but it is useful for refutation only.
18   For example, suppose some man | wishes to demonstrate that "The world is created of pre-existing substance", and he takes as demonstrative evidence for this that he saw
19 | a wall created from a substance, and that animals are created from a substance, and that the sky (heavens) have
20 a similarity to | the animals in that they are both corporeal. [Suppose] he wishes to make an inference by this "[argument
21 from] evidence to the absent", which he wishes | to render true this judgment about it [i.e., the absent, namely the heavens], on the basis of this resemblance [with a wall or the animals], namely that they are both corporeal.
270 || Then it is necessary, first of all, to demonstrate that the corporeality in respect to which the sky and animals are
2 similar be relevant to | the status of the animals as created from [pre-existing] substance. Now this [requires] that it
3 be true that "Everything bodied is | created from a substance which preceeded it". But if he wished to establish
4 this to be true, then he has [first] to | "investigate" all of the

---

[15] Cf. 266: 15 and 268: 13.
[16] I suppose *w-j-b* for the *w-h-b* of M. Türker's text.

kinds of corporeal substances until he has finished with all of them. [But] this is not possible without his "investigating"
5 amongst them | the sky also. For if that were not possible for him, then he could not establish the truth of "Every
6 (corporeal) body is created from | a substance". And if this is not shown to be true, then it is not possible to demonstrate
7 that "If the sky is corporeal, then it is created | from [pre-existing] substance".[17]

Now as regards refutation, it can be achieved by this
8 method alone. Suppose someone believes | that "Every change is from one thing to another", and consequently he "investigates" the [various] species of changes; and then he finds[18] that [coming into] being is a change from nothing
9 | into something, and that perishing is a change from something into nothing. By this [finding] it is refuted that
10 | "Every change is from one thing to another", due to the fact that [coming into] existence is a change, but not from
11 one thing to | another. For now [we have] an "arrangement" in the third figure, namely: "Every coming-to-be is
12 a change, and no single coming-to-be is from | one thing to another, so as a consequence not every change is from one thing to another".[19]

---

[17] Consider the argument pattern:

    Premiss 1: Certain (or even *All*) X's are Z's
    Premiss 2: All X's are Y's
    Conclusion: All Y's are Z's

or, in the concrete example:

    Certain members of the group G (viz., walls, animals) are brought into being from pre-existing substance.
    All members of the group G (walls, animals, the sky) are corporeal substances
    All corporeal substances—and thus in particular the sky—are brought into being from pre-existing substance

Al-Fārābī's objection to the argument is, very properly, that, as it stands, it is invalid.

[18] I suppose *w-j-d* for the *n-j-d* of M. Türker's text.

[19] The syllogism is EAO-3, Felapton. Al-Fārābī's point seems to

102   *Al-Fārābī's Short Commentary*

270   (iii) ANOTHER APPLICATION

13   It is possible to establish something as true | in another way, namely by examining the "matters" in which the
14   sensory evidence resembles "the absent", | or else into the other "matters" which characterize the sensory evidence
15   apart from this judgment. In either case, if | it ["the matter"] is "found" in some "thing", wherever it be, then the judgment is "found" [*ipso facto*].
16   For example, [suppose] that we examine | "contingent" things, [to see whether] if it ["contingency"] is "found" in some thing, wherever it be, then createdness is also "found".
17 | But the case is of this kind only if it is [true] that "Everything 'contingent' is created". Only if there is no difference
18   between saying | "Wherever one 'finds' the 'contingent' one
19   'finds' the created" and saying "Whatever | 'thing' is characterized by 'contingency', is also characterized by creation".
20   And this amounts to saying, | "Everything 'contingent' is created".

270   (iv) SUMMARIZING REMARKS

20   If this method [of reasoning by "investigation"] is correct, then it is [also] correct [to reason by] the "inference
271 || from evidence to the absent", and it is not possible to oppose [this mode of inference]. If it confined itself to
2   [holding] | that only what is "found" in the sensory evidence is "found" [in] the judgment, it does not necessarily follow,
3 | if something is "found" in the "absent" that this judgment[20] is actual; because it is only shown to be true by us

---

be this: Return to the argument pattern:

Premiss 1: Certain X's are Z's
Premiss 2: All X's are Y's

Conclusion: All Y's are Z's

But now suppose that Premiss 1 reports a negative finding: "This X is not a Z" or "No X is a Z". Now we can indeed infer the denial of the conclusion, i.e., not All Y's are Z's (by OAO-3 or EAO-3).

[20] That is, the judgment based on the sensory-evidence.

on Aristotle's 'Prior Analytics'

4 that the judgment follows if | it is "found" in the sensory evidence in question, and not otherwise.

5 And similarly [the "transfer"] is correct only when | it "finds" an actual judgment, unless it is known that it is

6 derived from an actual judgment. Because | if the situation is of this sort it is possible that some particular fact pertains to the sensory-evidence, but we do not know it, or it is bound

7 up with a condition | pertaining specifically to the "matter" [at hand in the evidence] which does not apply to the "absent", and the "transfer" is therefore not correct.

8 We have thus shown how it is possible | to draw true conclusions by this method [of "transfer"] and how it is not possible.

8-3. ESTABLISHING UNIVERSAL PREMISSES BY THE METHODS OF "RAISING" AND "FINDING"

271   (i) THE METHOD OF "RAISING"

8 Now as to the establishment of the truth [of the universal premiss of inference by "transfer"], we must inquire whether, if it [i.e., some "matter", presumably] is "raised",

9 | the judgment is [also] "raised" or not. For it is a very weak [conclusion] with regard to a thing if it is "raised".

10 | If one establishes a judgment by "raising", it does not necessarily result that when one "finds" this thing [which is "raised"] that one will "find" the judgment [to be true];

11 rather | it is the converse of this that is necessitated, namely if one "finds" the judgment; one "finds" [also] the thing [in question].[21]

---

[21] This discussion of inference by "raising" is complicated by the use of common words in technical senses. By "raising" is meant "to assume to be absent" (in the case of a quality) or "to assume to be false" (in the case of a judgment). By "finding" is meant the opposite, namely "to assume to be present" (in the case of a quality) or "to assume to be false" (in the case of a judgment). Given a judgment like "All men are animals", it can be said that the judgment "finds" a certain "thing" (viz., animality) in a certain "matter" (viz., man). Thus, since we have it as true that "All men are animals", it

12   For example, take the animals; if | one "raises" [this, viz., animality] from a thing, then one "raises" [also] from this thing that it is a man. But, it is not necessary that if one
13 "finds" an animal, | that one "finds" a man. Rather the matter lies with the converse, namely that if one "finds"
14 a man, it necessarily follows | that one "finds" an animal.

For such reasons it is not necessary that the applicability
15 of a judgment about all | of this "thing" is established as true by the fact that the judgment has been "raised" through the "raising" of the "thing".

However, when we wish to establish something to be true
16 | by the method of "raising", then it is necessary that we investigate whether if we "raise" the judgment we [also]
17 "raise" the "thing", or not. For if the "thing" | is "raised" by the "raising" of the judgment, then it necessarily follows if the "thing" is "found", that the judgment is "found" [also].
18 | We should [therefore] not cut short [our discussion] on these matters, without establishing the truth of whether, when the judgment is "raised", the "thing" is "raised" [also];
19 | for then it comes necessarily to follow that wherever the "thing" may be "found", the judgment is "found" also.[22]
20 It can be shown that | the matter is as we have said by means of a conditional syllogism in which the acceptance

---

follows that when dealing with some further "matter" X, that if we "raise" (as the "thing" at issue) animality, we *ipso facto* must "raise" being-a-man; and that if we "find" being-a-man, we must also "find" animality. These ideas are developed by al-Fārābī in the succeeding paragraph.

There does not seem to be much Aristotelian precedent for this treatment of "raising". I suppose that the basis is Aristotle's discussion of *aphairesis*. Cf. *Anal. Post.* 74a33–74b2, and cp. *Topica* 119a25–28; there seems to be no connection with the *anhairein* of *Topica* 120a13–15 and elsewhere.

[22] Consider the (true) judgment "All men are animals", attributing to the "matter" *man* the "thing" *animality*. If the judgment is "raised" (i.e., assumed to be false) then the "thing" is raised also (i.e., animality denied to man). On the other hand, if the "thing" animality is actually "found" in the "matter" man, then the judgment "All men are animals" is thereby also "found".

of the consequent is "excluded". For the "raising" of a judgment is nothing other than the denial of the judgment about the "matter", and similarly with the "raising" of a "thing". Thus if we put the "raising" of the judgment in place of the antecedent, and the "raising" of the "thing" in place of the consequent, and we thereupon "exclude" acceptance of the "raising" of the "thing" with this [exclusion] standing in place of the "exclusion" of acceptance of the consequent, [then] there necessarily follows the acceptance of what stands in place of the antecedent, namely the "finding" [as actually true] of the judgment.[23]

Thus, for example, if we wish to establish as true that "Every agent is corporeal", we inquire whether the corporeal is such that if one "raises" it, one [also] "raises" being-an-agent. If this is the situation, it is necessarily the case that "Every agent is corporeal", it being then posited that "whatever is not corporeal is not an agent". For if we "exclude" the acceptance of the consequent, namely that it-is-an-agent, it follows necessarily that it-is-corporeal. So it follows that whatever is an agent is corporeal.[24]

It is necessary to use this method in this way in order to establish the truth of a judgment about a "matter" which is supposed as a cause. We inquire whether when we make a judgment "raise", the "thing" "raises" [also]. If it were not true that when *corporeal substance* is "raised", then *agent* is raised also, then it would not follow by necessity

---

[23] Consider again a judgment ("All men are animals") attributing to a certain "matter" (men) a certain "thing" (animality). The relationship can be reformulated in conditional statement:

The judgment is true or false, according as "thing" is actually present in or absent from the "matter".

Clearly then if the judgment is "raised" (falsified) the "thing" is "raised" (assumed to be absent).

[24] The force of this example is to show that one can establish a universal statement by the method of "raising". To establish that "All X's are Y's" it suffices to show that when Y is "raised", X is also "raised".

that "Every agent is corporeal". And furthermore if, when *agent* is "raised", then *corporeal substance* is [also] "raised", then it would not follow that "Every agent is corporeal"; but rather it follows that "Every corporeal substance is an agent". And if neither the one nor the other is true, then there follows neither "Every agent is a corporeal substance" nor "Every corporeal substance is an agent".

(ii) THE JOINT METHOD OF "RAISING" AND "FINDING"

As regards the establishing as true [of a judgment] by the method of "finding" and "raising" together, it is better. [By this joint method], before a "thing" can be "raised", one must "raise" the judgment, and [before] it is "found" the judgment must be "found". It follows from the first that if the judgment is "found", the "thing" is "found" [also]. And it follows from the second that when the judgment is "raised", the "thing" is "raised" [also]. Thus it follows that the "thing" is characterized by the judgment, and the judgment by the "thing". The situation is as when, if *the neighing* is "raised", *the horse* is "raised", and when *the neighing* is "found", *the horse* is "found". Each of the two of them is convertible [viz., interchangeable] with the other in a [i.e., any] predication where it is specifically applicable.[25]

[But] there is no need in a syllogism for something which bears this predicate [viz., convertibility]. Thus when a premiss is universal, and is not convertible, then the

---

[25] That is, whenever *the horse* has some predicate, so does *the neighing*, and *vice versa*. In modern terminology, the two terms are *co-extensive*. The point is that two terms X and Y are related by the "joint method of 'raising' and 'finding' " when one of them is absent or present in an item according as the other is absent or present. When that is so, a particularly intimate relationship is established between being-X and being-Y, with the result that "All X's are Y's" and "All Y's are X's" are both validated.

syllogism can agree [in yielding a conclusion] just as though
21 it had one that | is convertible.²⁶

Before we can seek [for example] to show that "The world
22 is created, being corporeal", | it is first necessary for us to
establish that createdness is "found" in everything corporeal. Before we can seek || to establish as true that the
createdness of whatever thing is included within the cor-
2 poreal, it is [first] necessary that | we establish as true the
"finding" of corporeality in everything created.

[Furthermore] if we intended to prove [also] that corpo-
3 reality belongs to whatever | thing is included within the
created, then it would be necessary for us to establish as
4 true that both "Every | corporeal substance is created"
and "Every created thing is corporeal"; and then we would
wish to establish it as true both that createdness pertains to
5 whatever thing | is included within the corporeal, and also
that corporeality pertains to whatever thing is [included]
within the created.

6 However, if it is only | our intention to demonstrate the
createdness of whatever thing is included within the corporeal, just this alone [and no more], then it is only neces-
7 sary | that we establish it as true that "Every corporeal
substance is created". And if it were agreed that what we
have shown to be true is that "Every corporeal substance
8 is created", | then we would thereby have shown it to be
true [also] that "Every created thing is corporeal". It
cannot [thus] be shown to be true by us that "Every
9 corporeal substance | is created" from the truth of its
converse. [This is so] because it has already been shown
that an affirmative universal does not yield of its own truth
10 the truth | of its universal converse, but only its particular
converse.

11 Also, the corporeal does not become a cause | of the
"finding" (presence) of createdness if it converts with

---

²⁶ The universal premiss of a syllogism need only have the form
"All X's are Y's"; the concurrent existence of the converse relationship between X's and Y's is never a requisite.

108   *Al-Fārābī's Short Commentary*

createdness. Because this would require that the corporeal
12 be a cause, | but all that is shown to be true by it is the "finding" (presence) of createdness in whatever is [included] within the [realm of] the corporeal. It is sufficient for this
13 that it be shown true that | createdness pertains to every corporeal substance.[27]

273   (iii) SUMMARY

13   In this way it comes about that the establishment of the
14 universal premiss [by which | the "transfer of a judgment from the evidence to the absent" becomes possible] by the method of "finding" and "raising" combined, is the best.[28]
15 However, we may [sometimes] be satisfied | when something is shown to be true [by the method] that where the judgment is "found" one "finds" [also] the "thing" which
16 is supposed as the cause, wherever it be and in | whatever matter, in accordance with what we have said [above].

8-4. THE TYPES OF "TRANSFER"

273   (i) INTRODUCTION

17 | It is necessary that we investigate and examine if the sensory-evidence gives us evidence for a "matter"[29]
18 and shows the truth of | "finding" this [particular] "matter" in every "matter" generally in which the sensory-evidence
19 resembles the absent. When a "transfer | of a judgment from the observed sensory-evidence to the absent" is possible: (A) Is this because this sensory-evidence is service-
274 able, || and useful for true knowledge [in that] it truly "finds" the point of resemblance of the sensory-evidence to
2 the "matter" | which is supposed as the cause? Or (B) is

---

[27] Compare 268: 14 above.

[28] The whole long discussion of "raising" and "finding" is purely ancillary to the discussion of inference by "transfer". Its purpose is to show how the universal premiss on which a "transfer" must rest is to be established.

[29] Literally: *the sensory-evidence if it gives us evidence.*

this only because it is true that the "finding" of the judg-
3 ment about all of the "matter" which is supposed | as the
cause takes some other form, without the "matter" of the
sensory-evidence in the judgment being serviceable for
4 showing the truth | of the judgment when it [viz., the
"matter"] is supposed as the cause?

Both of these ways have been the subject of discourse
[i.e., both of these alternatives have been maintained].
5 [But] we say that if it[i.e., the sensory-evidence] is | service-
able, then this is one of two ways:

(ii) THE FIRST WAY

5   Either, [i.e., first] if we make the sensory-evidence by
6 itself the middle term, and [the argument] is composed | in
the third figure. For example: "This builder is an agent,
and he is corporeal, so it follows from this that the agent
7 is corporeal." | Although it does not follow as necessary
that *every* agent is corporeal, yet some agent is corporeal.
8   Since | categorical propositions are sometimes formulated
loosely, being taken as though they have universal quantity-
indicators, the categorical conclusions [from such premises]
9 come to be conceived | as of the status of having their
quantity-indicators universal [also]. This is especially so
10 when the formulation of the categorical statements | is by
the "THE" [i.e., the definite article] with a term. For
example, when one says "The agent is corporeal", then the
"THE" with a term in this [formulation] give the im-
11 pression that | "*Every* agent is corporeal", since the "THE"
with a term is frequently used instead of the expression
12 | "all".

So in this way and in this manner, and to this extent, it
13 is possible that the sensory-evidence be serviceable | for
showing the truth of the "finding" of a judgment about a
"matter" which is supposed as the cause. Namely—that it
14 yields [a conclusion] which is truth [about] | a particular part,
but is loosely construed, and it is taken [as] a categorical

15 conclusion [of universal form]. Then[30] | the "THE" with a term is used in its formulation, so that it gives the impression of universality in a judgment about the whole
16 of the "matter" which | is supposed as the cause.[31]

(iii) THE SECOND WAY

17 | The other [i.e., second] way is to make the sensory-evidence the middle term in [a syllogism of] the first figure.
18 For example, | if we wish to establish as true that "Every agent is corporeal", we examine the "things" which are
19 | included within the agent, namely the tailor and the builder [and so on]. Then we find that every one of them is corporeal. Consequently we think that it is thereby necessary
275 || that "Every agent is corporeal"; since the tailor and the builder become intermediaries [i.e., a middle term] between
2 | the agent and the corporeal, in the same way in which the species of agents become the middle term in induction.
3 | Thus [the argument] is composed as follows: "The agent is a builder, and the builder is corporeal, so the agent is
4 corporeal". And so the builder stands in place | of the species of agents, as though all or the majority of them had been "investigated". It is as though one had exhausted
5 | the "investigation" of the species of agents by [checking] one or two of them only, and this [part] stands in place of the
6 totality | or the majority.

Consequently there is a looseness in the universality, and in its formulation by a categorical [statement (of universal

---

[30] I suppose f for q.

[31] This is a luke-warm defense of the "serviceability" of the argument by "transfer". As al-Fārābī explains it, the argument has a valid basis of the form:

(All) X's are Y's
(Some or All) X's are Z's
―――――――――――――――
Therefore, (Some) Y's are Z's

But now an improper conclusion is substituted by construing the quantitatively indefinite, but actually particular conclusion of this third-figure syllogism to be universal.

on Aristotle's 'Prior Analytics' 111

type)]. Thus it is said: "The agent is the tailor, and the
builder, | and the shoemaker and the carpenter; and all of
these are corporeal, so it follows that the agent is cor-
poreal". Thereupon it is imagined | that this is a [universal]
categorical in the conclusion. The "THE" with a term is
[again] used [to say] that "Every agent is corporeal". | But
this usage is equivocal [between a universal and a particular
construction].[32]

(iv) SUMMARY

In these two ways it is possible for the sensory-evidence
to be serviceable in | showing the truth of a judgment about
a "matter" which is supposed as the cause.[33] These, then,
are the ways which are customarily[34] | used for showing the
truth of the [universal] premiss by which the "inference from
evidence to the absent" comes about.[35]

---

[32] Thus the "second way" is no more capable of warranting a universal conclusion than the first. Its seeming persuasiveness, al-Fārābī argues, derives solely in the equivocation in the quantity of definite-article propositions.

[33] It is difficult to see how, having shown them to be fallacious, al-Fārābī can claim that these two modes of reasoning are "serviceable". But it is significant that he uses a colloquial word, not some technical term of logic like "valid", etc. He seemingly intends to suggest that such reasonings are "useful in everyday discourse" as contrasted with reasonings which are "demonstrative of scientific conclusions".

[34] Customarily, but not strictly speaking correctly.

[35] The ultimate basis for this treatment of "transfer" (i.e., analogy) is *Anal. Pr.* II, 25; however, al-Fārābī's discussion goes far beyond this basis in both detail and precision.

Section 9

THE "FOUR PRINCIPLES" FOR ESTABLISHING STATEMENTS

INTRODUCTION

| Let us now speak about the *special principles* of the [four syllogistic] "arts" which warrant the acceptance | of statements. These are the principles from which the statements are composed which Aristotle called | "convincing syllogisms", and which are mentioned at the end of his book called *Prior Analytics*. | He says that they go back to[1] the syllogisms which he enumerated in the first part of that book. | These are his words in the text: "Not only the dialectical and the demonstrative syllogisms are [characterized] by the figures | which were spoken about, but also the rhetorical and the 'convincing'."[2] These principles are four: (i) [the first] of them is the universal || which it is stipulated to be a universal, (ii) [the second] of them is the universal which is substituted for an intended particular, | (iii) [the third] of them is the particular which is substituted for an intended universal, and (iv) [the fourth] of them is the example [i.e., a particular substituted for a particular].[3]

---

[1] Or: *are reducible to.*

[2] *Anal. Pr.* 68b10–13 (and cf. *Topica*, 100a27). Instead of speaking "convincing syllogisms" the Greek speaks of *haplōs hētisoun pistis* "any attempt to produce conviction".

[3] Cf. *Anal. Pr.* 69a14–19. These lead to the syllogistic arguments appropriate to the last four of the five "syllogistic arts": viz., scientific, dialectical, sophistical, rhetorical, and "exemplary" (or poetical) syllogisms. Al-Fārābī appears to group the last four types of syllogisms together as "convincing" to contrast, as a group, with the properly "scientific syllogisms".

9-1. UNIVERSAL SUBSTITUTED FOR UNIVERSAL

3 | As regards the universal which is stipulated as universal, it is a premiss which is accepted as universal, from which
4 a judgment is "transferred" | to a "thing", which shows it to be true that it [i.e., the "thing"] is included within the subject of this premiss. For example [consider the state-
5 ment], "Every wine | is prohibited".[4] This premiss is accepted as universal. And therefore, when it is true of
6 something that it is | wine, one [thereby] judges a prohibition upon it. Now this "transfer" is [achieved] by a
7 syllogism composed in the figure namely: | "Every wine is prohibited, and this [fluid] which is in the jug is wine, so it follows that what is in the jug is prohibited".[5]

8 | Some of these statements accepted [as universal] may be formulated by an assertoric proposition such as "Every
9 intoxicant is forbidden". Some | may be formulated in other [types of] statements which have the force of assertoric propositions, such as statements of permission, pro-
10 hibition, | urging, restraining, command, and interdiction. As examples, [take] the statement of the Koran,[6] "Avoid
11 untruth",[7] | and the Koranic statements,[8] "Wash your faces",[9] and "When you speak be just",[10] and "Fulfill your

[4] Cf. *Koran, Al-mā'idah* ("The Table"), 5: 90–91.
[5] The terminology and the reasoning here are as follows: We "accept as universal" the premiss, "All X (wine) is Y (prohibited)". Given now some "thing" Z (this fluid) which is "included within the subject" of the given premiss—so that "All Z is X"—we "transfer" the predicate of the premiss to this "thing" by the AAA-1 (Barbara) syllogism:

$$\frac{\text{All X is Y}}{\text{All Z is X}}$$
$$\text{All Z is Y}$$

[6] Literally: *of the All-powerful and All-mighty*.
[7] *Al-ḥajj* ("The Pilgrimage"), 22: 30.
[8] Literally: *the statement of the All-high*.
[9] *Al-mā'idah* ("The Table"), 5: 8.
[10] *Al-anʿ-ām* ("Cattle"), 6: 151.

12 | commitments".[11] Thus when we have [universally] accepted [premisses] formulated in statements that are not
13 assertoric, and we wish to | make use of them as premisses in syllogisms, then it is necessary to substitute assertoric
14 statements in their place. For example, | if we were told "Avoid wine", and we want to use this statement as part
15 of a syllogism, then it is necessary to | substitute in its place[12] the statement "Every wine is to-be-avoided", or "It [i.e., wine] is necessarily to be avoided".
16 | The subjects and predicates of these [premisses] can be
17 formulated by nouns which are called | *univocal*. They may also be formulated by nouns which are called *equivocal*. The
18 noun called *univocal* | is one which embraces many things and refers to one common meaning common to all of them.
19 An *equivocal* noun is one which embraces | many things but does *not* refer to one common meaning common to all of them. Now a [statement] accepted [as universal] can
277 only occur when the universal premisses || are such that their formulation contains as subjects and predicates the so-
2 called univocal nouns. | As regards those [premisses] whose formulation contains equivocal nouns, these are only thought to be universal [statements], but they are not
3 universal [statements] | in actual truth.

9·2. UNIVERSAL SUBSTITUTED FOR PARTICULAR

4 | As for the universal which is substituted for an intended particular, it is a premiss accepted as universal [but] sub-
5 stituted | in place of a particular premiss. It occurs when the intention of the speaker is something particular, but he enunciates this particular by a general and universal state-
6 ment | and his intention [in the universal statement] is the
7 particular. A man says: "There is no good in friends | nor in children". But he [actually] only means some of them.

---

[11] *Al-mā'idah* ("The Table"), 5: 1.
[12] I suppose *m-kā-n-h* for the *f-k-'-nn-h* of M. Türker's text.

Or similarly [he says]: "People deny the prophets",[13] meaning some of them only.

If it happens that we have an accepted universal, and we know that its intention was some particular part [only], and we know [specifically] which particular part was intended, then we would take this part [and would formulate the statement about it, instead of the misleading universal]. If this part were also universal for some other thing, then we would take it and use it as the aforementioned universal is used. For anything whatever that is rendered true by being included within this specialized universal, we [simply] "transfer" the judgment which was judged [previously] about it [viz., the more general universal], to this more special [universal].[14]

For example, among the accepted universals we have: "It is necessary to cut off the hand of the thief".[15] This [universal] is substituted in place of a part of those who do thieving, namely the thief of [something whose value is at least] a quarter of a dinar. Thus [the term] *the thief* is taken in this way when the cutting-off of the hand is judged about it, and so we obtain a universal premiss. Therefore, if it is true that Zaid is a thief, and it is in this way necessary that his hand be cut, then this also is [the result of] a syllogism composed in the first figure.[16]

Many universals which are found in the place of particulars pertain to particulars which intend certain particulars

---

[13] Cf. *Koran, Ya Sīn*, 36: 29; etc.

[14] Thus if the original (careless) universal was "Dogs are long" *meaning* "Dachshunds are long", then we can *transfer* the original statement from dogs-in-general to dachshunds-in-particular by the AAA-1 (Barbara) syllogism:

> [All] dogs are long
> All Dachshunds are dogs
> ―――――――――――――
> All Dachshunds are long

[15] Cf. *Koran, Al-mā'idah* ("The Table"), 5: 38.

[16] This argument again conforms to the pattern of an AAA-1 (Barbara) syllogism.

18 that are at the outset | not contemplated [at all]. The majority of them are concealed at the outset, so that one does not know whether they have been substituted for a
19 particular or not, | and it is not [even] known that they have been substituted for a particular. Frequently it is concealed
20 which particular it is, so that it is not known which | thing it is. Thus, when it is concealed, then it is necessary that one seek to know it through a syllogism composed in the
278 ways we have discussed [above]. || Then, if this particular is [known] by us by a syllogism, then we obtain a universal premiss. Then we use it [viz., the universal premiss] in
2 | the same way we used the other universals.

9-3. PARTICULAR SUBSTITUTED FOR UNIVERSAL

3 | As regards the substitution of a particular for a universal, this comes about when there is a statement which [actually]
4 intends some [entire] "matter", | but some particular [part] of this "matter" is substituted for the "matter" [itself]. It results that whatever is attributed to this [particular] part
5 consequently | is [to be] attributed to the universal. For example [consider] the statement "A certain person does no wrong, not even to the weight of a single grain",[17] meaning
6 not even in | a very little thing. [Here] we substitute some [portion] of the small things, namely the weight of a single grain, in place of the unqualifiedly small.
7 | Thus let there be a statement about motion, and change the statement to be about something which is one particular
8 species | of motion. The result is that what is attributed to the "thing" which is the species, is to be attributed [generally] to every motion.
9 In | this way, when a certain "matter" accords with the accepted [statements], a judgment is judged about it [i.e.,
10 the "matter"], and it is taken as substitute for | some universal; and [if] we know what universal that is, [then] we make this judgment [about the "matter"] attributable

[17] Cf. Koran, Al-anbayāt ("The Prophets"), 21: 46.

11 to that universal. | Thus we obtain a universal premiss.
12 And so it is used as one would use the premisses that | were accepted about the initial "matter", in general; just like the two kinds mentioned above.
13   For example, it is among | the accepted [statements] which we have that, "It is prohibited to say 'fie' to one's
14 parents".[18] This [injunction] was not intended | to prohibit this particular word alone but was intended to prohibit words of this sort generally, i.e., [every] refractoriness
15 | towards parents. If we know that it intends this universal,
16 we obtain a universal premiss, | namely "[Every] refractoriness towards parents is prohibited". And then if when is shown that some certain thing is refractoriness towards
17 parents, then one judges about it | that it is evil. This [resulting] syllogism is composed in the first figure.[19]
18 | When we arrive at some "matter" which is judged about by some judgment, but we do not know whether [we are entitled] to substitute for it [i.e., for the "matter"] some
19 universal, | or not to make any [such] substitution at all— either because the intention which is itself present in the judgment is not universal, or because although we do know
279 that it [i.e., the "matter"] has been || substituted in place of some universal, or there are many possible universals, and we do not know which one we want for the substituted
2 "matter"—| then it is not possible for us to "transfer" the judgment about that "matter" to something which is not [specifically] included within this "matter". Rather, we
3 can [then] "transfer" | the judgment only to the particulars which are included within it [i.e., the "matter"]. When [however], we know that it [i.e., the "matter"] is substituted
4 for some universal, and we know which | universal this is, [then] we can "transfer" this judgment to some other "matter" which is associated with the first "matter" in this universal.
5 | As to how can we know that this "matter" has been

---

[18] *Koran, Al-isrā'* ("The Night-Journey"), 17: 22.
[19] Again, it is clearly an AAA-1 (Barbara).

substituted in place of a universal, or [has] not, and if it has been substituted | which universal it is which stands in its place [the situation is as follows]: This is sometimes known of itself [i.e., is self-evident], and is not reached by discursive reasoning. | And [in the case of] that which is *not* known of itself, it is necessary to seek knowledge about it by a syllogism composed according to one of the ways [of composition] which | we discussed in what has preceded, or else we must use for it the methods treated in [the discussion of] "inference | from evidence to the absent". For it has been shown by us that a universal can only be substituted in place of a particular if | that judgment [about the particular] has been shown to be true about every one of the universals which belong to that particular, as in the "inference from evidence | to the absent".[20]

The most trustworthy way in which it is possible to show some "matter" to be true of such a universal | is that we show this to be true by one of the syllogistic figures which we have discussed [above]. But as for showing something to be true by the method | of "investigating" [21] its state here is just like the state in "inference from evidence to the absent".[22] This is so | in that we refer to[23] the "matter" about which it judges some judgment, and that we take the universals of this | "matter", and then "investigate" the particulars of every one of these universals; and then if the universal [in question] is "found" in the totality of the particulars | belonging to this judgment, then it has been shown true that this universal is what was intended by this "matter", and that this "matter" | has only been substituted in place of that universal.

Thus it is evident that if we do this [substitution], then we [must] already know the truth of this judgment | with respect to whatever falls under that universal, before we

---

[20] Compare 266: 7-9, and 269: 1-9 above.
[21] That is, by *induction*. Cf. 264: 5-14.
[22] See Section 8-2.
[23] I suppose *n-ʿ-m-d* for the *t-ʿ-m-d* of M. Türker's text.

[can] know the truth of the judgment about this universal [itself].

19 Thus if it be our aim only | to show the truth of that judgment about that universal in order to know that judgment to be true with respect to some [particular] part 20 | which falls under that universal, then it is clear that, if we take this step, then it is not necessary for us, after that, 21 to | "transfer" this judgment from this universal to something that falls under it; if we [must] already know the truth 22 of this | judgment with respect to every one of the items falling under that universal, before we can know about its 280 truth with respect to that universal [itself]. For if || it be the case that when we "investigate" the particulars one by one, it does not at all become evident to us by this "investi- 2 gation" that this judgment is true | about certain of the particulars of the universal, and [yet] we do not know of 3 which of them it is to be negated, then it is evident | that it is not possible for us to make this judgment about something belonging to that universal, neither that it is thus-and-so 4 nor | that it is not thus-and-so.[24]

If, when we "investigate" them we find that some of the 5 particulars of a certain universal do not admit | of the "finding" of that judgment, then it becomes evident by this that this judgment does not hold for the totality of that 6 universal. | Thus, as has already been shown, this method is not serviceable for showing the truth of a universal [judgment]; [although] it is very serviceable for refut- 7 ing one.[25] For | [suppose] someone thinks, regarding some universal, that it is to be substituted in place of some particular "matter", and so judges some judgment about 8 it. | So we investigate what falls under this universal, and find that some of its particulars do not admit of the "find- 9 ing" of this judgment [about them]. | The composition of this form [of reasoning] is a syllogism in the third figure,

---

[24] That is, we can make neither a universally affirmative nor a universally negative judgment.

[25] See 265: 15–266: 11, and 268: 19–270: 7 above.

10 and it necessitates | the refutation of the universality of that judgment.[26] We have already explained this in the section
11 on "inference from evidence to | the absent".[27] This method here is like that of "deriving[28] a judgment which renders necessary the cause from the effects".[29]
12 | As to the other ways in which it is possible to show some "matter" to be true of a universal, such as "finding",
13 | "raising" and others, these have also been elucidated in that section.[30]

An example of this [is as follows]. It is among the accepted
14 [statements] which | are given us that "The selling of wheat for wheat in unequal quantities is prohibited".[30a] Thus it
15 is necessary that we know whether | there is intended by this judgment wheat alone, or whether some universal is
16 to be substituted—be it *the edible,* | or *the measurable,* or some other universal—and to be put in its place [i.e.,
17 in place of wheat]. If [something else] is intended, | be it the edible or the measurable or some other universal, then
18 the particular is uttered, but | that universal is intended by what is uttered. But then it is necessary[31] that we already know that it has been substituted for a universal,
19 | unless it be that wheat belongs to many universals—

[26] Let the initial judgment be "All the X's are Y's". Let Z be the universal that is thought to be substituted in place of the X's here, so that "All X's are Z's" is true, and "All Z's are Y's" is *sub judice*. Suppose further that the W's for which "All W's are Z's" is true, are such that *not* all the W's are Y's so that we have "Some W's are not Y's". Then we have the syllogism:

Some W's are not Y's
All W's are Z's
―――――――――――――
Some Z's are not Y's

This third-figure syllogism (OAO-3, Bokardo) establishes the contradictory of the statement under inquiry.

[27] Namely Section 8 above.
[28] I suppose '-j-r-ā-' for '-j-z-ā-' as in 269: 11 above.
[29] See 269: 10 and following.
[30] See above, 271: 8 and following.
[30a] Cf. Schacht, *Origins of Muhammedan Jurisprudence*, pp. 67, etc.
[31] I suppose l-'-z-m for the l-n-n-z-l of M. Türker's text.

281 such as the edible or the measurable—and || then we do not know whether to substitute, in place of wheat, the measurable or the edible or something else. Then it is not
2 possible | to "transfer" the prohibition [from wheat to something else], [but] only to something which is included within wheat as a species of it.
3 | But how are we to know whether wheat has been substituted in place of one of its universals or which universal
4 | is to be substituted in its place?

In many cases of this sort, we know by its being self-
5 evident, without | discursive reasoning, that by it [i.e., the particular] a universal is intended. For example, we know
6 [this] in the dictum of the Koran:[32] "God | does no injustice to the weight of a single grain". [33]

Whatever is not known as self-evident—as in the example
7 of the wheat—it is necessary | to seek to attain [knowledge of] it by a syllogism composed in one of the ways which we have discussed [above]. It [i.e., syllogism] will only
8 make evident | to us the universal which has been substituted in place of wheat, when the judgment is true about
9 some universal that the prohibition holds for | the whole of it [i.e., the universal], such as [the whole of] the edible or the measurable. Thus when it has been shown to be true that, "Everything edible is such that inequality in it is
10 forbidden", | or "Everything measurable is of this sort", then it has been shown that the universal which is sub-
11 stituted in place of the wheat | is the edible or the measurable [respectively].

If this [judgment about the universal] has been shown to be true by the method of "investigation",[34] the situation will be as follows:
12 Namely, | we take the greater universal—such as the edible for example, or the measurable—and then we "in-
13 vestigate" the species | of the measurable and the species of

[32] Literally: *of God, the All-mighty and the All-high.*
[33] *Al-nisā'* ("The Women"), 4: 39.
[34] That is, by induction. See Section 7 above.

the edible. Now if either of these two is such that the prohibition is true of [all] its species, then that will be the universal | which is to be substituted in place of it [i.e., the wheat].³⁵

Suppose we discover that it [i.e., the judgment of prohibition] is true about [all] the species of the measurable. Then, if this be so, then we must already know | the truth of the prohibition about every one of the species of the measurable, before we know that the measurable [itself] is prohibited. And so we know | now that rice is [also] prohibited, on account of our knowledge that everything measurable is prohibited. This is so [because] | when we "investigated" it, it was only our wish to show the judgment to be true about the measurable in order to know the truth of the judgment about | something contained within the measurable, namely rice, for example. Thus it is not necessary for us to "transfer" the prohibition from || the measurable to the rice, if, when we know the truth of the prohibition about rice, | we already know about the prohibition of the measurable [since this includes rice]. This must be the situation if we "investigate" rice as one of the species of the measurable which we are "investigating".³⁶

| [However, if] rice remains unknown [with respect to] the judgment [regarding prohibition], then it will not be possible for us to [infer by] "transfer" that "Everything | measurable is prohibited", if there is among the measurable things something [viz., rice] that has not been "investigated". And then it is [not!]³⁷ known whether it [viz., the total universal] is prohibited or not. | If it were the case that when we "investigate" it, we [still] do not know whether

---

³⁵ We now obtain the AAA-1 (Barbara) syllogism:

All (say) the measurable is prohibited
All wheat is measurable
———————————————
All wheat is prohibited

³⁶ For then the conclusion can be obtained syllogistically, without any "transfer".

³⁷ This insertion is obviously required by the sense.

the totality of the species are prohibited or not, then it is
not possible for us | to make a judgment about it [viz.,
this totality], neither that every measurable is prohibited
nor that it is not prohibited. We are stopped [at this point]
unless | this [viz., that all the species are prohibited] is
shown by us to be so.

But if someone maintains that "Everything measurable is
prohibited", and so we "investigate" the species | of the
measurable, and find that some of these species are not
prohibited—like the peas, for example—then it is refuted
that it is the case that | "Everything measurable is prohibited". This [reasoning] is such that its syllogism is
composed in the third figure; namely [as follows]: "Peas are
| measurable, and peas are not prohibited, thus not everything measurable is prohibited". [38]

| It has thus been shown that this method [viz., "investigation"] is not serviceable for demonstrating the truth [of
a judgment about a universal], but that it is serviceable for
refutation.

However, | the [important] point in these things is, as
Aristotle said, that it is not necessary | to seek exactness
in everything to the same extent; but that the exactness of
every | thing must be in proportion to its subject-matter.[39]
It is necessary to attain exactness | in each [subject]
matter to the degree of its capacity for this [viz., exactness],
and it is not the capacity of everything that one can attain
| complete certainty in it. Rather, it is sufficient in many
matters to limit oneself to | knowledge that is without
[absolute] certainty. Aristotle himself says that to seek
exactness in every | thing to the same extent is the act of
one lacking experience in giving demonstrations for everything.[40]

|| In this [subject] there manifests itself something which
[also] manifests itself in actions and dealings and partnerships

---

[38] The syllogism is EAO-3 (Felapton).
[39] *Nicomachean Ethics*, 1094b12 and following.
[40] *Ibid.*, 1094b24-27.

2 [in human affairs], | and this is [indicated] in the [saying] which has come down, which says: "Exactness is
3 disunion". For by exactness we may attain here | the very opposite of what we intend [to attain] by it. Exactness in the matter of the syllogism is of just this kind. For that
4 which is attained by it | is the very opposite of what the intention of the syllogism is. For the syllogism only intends to show something and to remove doubt and uncertainty.
5 | But if the matter of a syllogism is made more exact in
6 some matters than is suitable for them, | it may come about that nothing is shown by it at all.

7 As for [a subject] in which | laxity[41] is used in [obtaining] knowledge and [complete] exactness is abandoned, this can be very serviceable in the "convincing" [syllogistic] "art",
8 and in many | of the other [syllogistic] "arts".[42] For the [syllogistic "arts"] similar to these use a great deal of laxity
9 for the knowledge they provide. It is necessary | not to surpass in these matters the [syllogistic] arts [with respect to exactness], for only if[43] it [viz., leniency] is used in them can they be of much service. But if [exactness] is extended
10 to | the other [disciplines, i.e., those in which exactness is not appropriate,] then they will either not attain their
11 intention at all, or it will become with them | as we said,[44] [that one attains] the very opposite of what is intended.

For these reasons, the method of "investigation" may be
12 | suitable for showing something to be true in such [syllogistic] "arts", if one "investigates" [only] most [rather than
13 strictly all] of the things | which fall under the universal [at issue].

Not only this, but also if the things which fall under the
14 universal are "investigated", and one does not | "find" the

---

[41] The word which I render as "laxity" throughout could equally well, or even better, be translated as "generosity".

[42] See 275: 12–276: 2 above. Regarding the "syllogistic arts", see M. Steinschneider, *Al-Farabi*, pp. 17–18; and R. Walzer, *Greek into Arabic*, pp. 130–135.

[43] I suppose *innamā* for the *innahā* of M. Türker's text.

[44] See 283: 2–3 above.

judgment, it being inapplicable in every one of them, then this may also prove sufficient for establishing the truth [of the appropriate negative judgment]. | This may happen if but a few of them are "investigated", [even] one or two [only].

16   Similarly, the other ways | which were adopted for showing a universal [judgment] to be true—such as the methods of "finding" and of "raising" and others—they [also] are extremely useful | in cases belonging to these [syllogistic] "arts". And if any of the inexact [methods] are adopted at all, then it may well prove necessary || with them [i.e., for these other methods also] to adopt inexactness in every instance, as has already proven necessary in many branches of knowledge.

9-4. "EXAMPLE" (i.e., PARTICULAR SUBSTITUTED FOR PARTICULAR)

| *"Example"* occurs when two "matters" are taken that resemble each other [in some way], about one of which [something] is judged to the effect that it is characterized by some "thing" | which is to be a resemblance with the other "matter", and there is silence about this other.[45]

---

[45] The technical terminology of "example" is somewhat complex. We have:
   (i) Two "matters", A and B
  (ii) A "thing" T which constitutes the point of resemblance between A and B
 (iii) A "judgment", known to obtain about one of the two matters, say A, but with regard to whose applicability to the other, viz. B, we are not informed.

Given such a situation, the inference by "example" consists in arguing that, since the two "matters" A and B resemble one another with respect to the "thing" which is a point of similarity between them, B will *also* resemble A with respect to the applicability of what the "judgment" in question affirms of A. A here serves as the "example" for the "other matter" B. The reasoning has the pattern:

$$\begin{array}{l} \text{This A and this B are both T's} \\ \underline{\text{This A is a C}} \\ \therefore \text{ This B is a C} \end{array}$$

That one of the two about which the judgment is known
is the *example* for the one about which the judgment is not
known. Thus [in inference by "example"] the judgment
which was judged about it [viz., the known example] is
transferred to the other, resembling ["matter"]. But one can
know that the judgment which is judged about one of the
two ["matters"] is [correctly] judged to be a "thing" which
is a [point of] resemblance between the two ["matters"],
only if it has been shown by us to be true that this judgment is [correct] about this "thing" which is the [point of]
resemblance between them [viz., the two "matters"].

When it is the case that this "matter" which is treated
by the judgment is as though it has been substituted for
the "thing" which is the [point of] resemblance, then
"example" is almost identical with a connection between
the particular "matter" which is put in place of a universal,
and [then] one knows the truth of the judgment about the
"thing" which is the [point of] resemblance in the [same]
way in which a universal is known which is put in place of
a particular. If this is shown to be true, one obtains a
universal premiss. And if it is shown that something is
included within the subject of this [universal] premiss,
[then] the judgment which was judged about it [i.e., the
universal] would be "transferred" by the [reasoning by]
"example" to that [particular] thing. The syllogism [for
this reasoning] is composed in the first figure.[46]

The example mentioned in the section preceding this
one should properly be [discussed][47] here. For wheat is

---

[46] The reasoning is now changed from the pattern of the foregoing footnote to the pattern:
Since "This A is a T" and "This A is a C", it would seem that "All T's are C's". Thus:

All T's are C's
This B is a T

This B is a C

This syllogism is an AAA-1 (Barbara).

[47] See 280: 13–282: 10.

only exemplary for rice when it is shown true that the prohibition is only judged about it [i.e., rice] in view of
14 | the "thing" which is a [point of] resemblance between rice and wheat, namely, edibility or measurability [for instance].
15 But a "thing" is shown | by us to be that in view of which some judgment which is made about it [i.e., a matter] only when it [i.e., the judgment] is shown true regarding [*everything* involved;] in the present instance[48] that every edible
16 whatsoever or | every measurable whatsoever are prohibited. The truth of this can be derived by the methods
17 by which one discovers | that a universal is to be substituted in place of a particular, and by these methods pre-eminently.[48a]
18 | It is necessary to practice laxity to some extent in showing the truth of a universal [judgment] in these [syllogistic]
19 "arts". Otherwise, | one will not attain the intended [goal]. Thus the matter in which the example resembles the other
20 "matter" may be | only represented in the imagination, without the example [actually known to have this resemblance], so that a universal premiss is obtained from that,
285 and from the judgment which || is judged about the example. Thus if it is shown regarding some "thing" that
2 it is included within the subject | of that [universal] premiss, the judgment regarding the example is [immediately] "transferred" to that "thing".[49] And in a [case] of this sort, there would be no doubt about it that the "transfer"
3 | was made only from the example to what resembles it, yet [also] no doubt that the example is dispensable in [this]
4 "transfer" to what is similar.[50] But one can | dispense with it [i.e., "example"] only when there is a universal premiss which is "transferred" from a judgment, and [even then] only

[48] I suppose '-*y* for the '-*w* of M. Türker's text.
[48a] See 278: 3 and following.
[49] Note, that throughout this paragraph the words "thing" and "matter" are *interchanged* with respect to their role in the preceding discussion.
[50] Since, in such a case of actual inclusion, the conclusion can be reached syllogistically, and no reasoning by "example" is required.

in the "matter" which constitutes the [point of] resemblance. Also it may not | be thought that the truth of the judgment about the example is dispensable in showing the truth of this judgment about the "matter" | in which the example resembles the other "thing".

It is possible to find [in some cases] that the "matter" respecting which the resemblance [with the example] obtains is | [actually] conjoined with[51] the example, and is not separated from it. But [in other cases] it [i.e., the "matter"] is [merely] imagined in the mind as connected with the example, so that | the judgment about the "thing" in respect to which the resemblance obtains is [accepted as] true, it [i.e., the "matter"] being [thus] connected with the example [in imagination].[52] If [the case] be | of this sort, one does not in actuality attain a universal premiss at all, but [rather] the premiss | for an [inference by] "example", which is particular, except that the force of this premiss is the force of a universal premiss, so that it renders true, | for this reason, a "transfer" to the "matter" which falls under the "thing" in respect to which | its resemblance [to the example] obtains. Then, it is thought regarding this "transfer" that it [goes] from the example to that which resembles it, and that it is [thus] from a particular to a particular, | not from a universal to a particular, like something which conforms to the case of a syllogism. For this reason it is thought that inference by "example" | does not [take place] by a syllogism.[53]

---

[51] Literally: *is not detached from*.

[52] There are thus two species of inference by "example", viz., as will be seen below, inference by "example" proper on the one hand, and inference by universalized "example" on the other.

[53] There are thus two types of "inference by example", viz.:
(i) Inference by "example" *proper*, whose pattern (using the conventions introduced in footnote 45 above) is:

This A is a T
This A is a C
This B is a T
∴ This B is a C

Consequently [we have] what Aristotle said about "example": "It is a thing not as whole | to part, and not as part to whole, but as part to part".[54] The "transfer" in "example" | is not [however] a "transfer" from a particular simply without any universal, and it is also not in a universal simply, | without any particular, but it is from a particular connected with a universal or a universal connected with a particular. For this reason, | this particular becomes like a universal and this universal like a particular. From this standpoint it is evident that Aristotle | did not maintain that a universal premiss, if [actually] isolated from the example, can then be "transferred" from it [i.e., the example] to something which falls under | the subject of the premiss in a "transfer" by "example". But he maintained that inference by "example" [proper], and "transfer" by [a universalized] "example" are | two kinds [of inference] such as we have outlined.[55] He said that the latter is strictly a syllogism, and that the former | does not take place by a syllogism, but has the force of a syllogism. This former kind [of inference, viz., inference by "example" proper] is the one in which the [inference by] "example" must[56] dispense | with a "transfer", because it shows directly by an "example" the truth of the judgment about the "matter" which has the resemblance | [that obtains between] the example and something else. So this "matter" becomes the intermediary [i.e., the middle term] between

---

(ii) Inference by a *universalized* "example", or "example by transfer", whose pattern is

All T's are C's (since A, which is a T, is also a C)
This B is a T
‾‾‾‾‾‾‾‾‾‾‾‾
This B is a C

The universalized inference by "example" answers to an AAA-1 (Barbara) syllogism, but inference by "example" proper is not syllogistic.

[54] *Anal. Pr.* 69a14–16.
[55] See 285: 6 ff. But where did Aristotle draw this distinction?
[56] I suppose *w-j-b* for the *w-j-d* of M. Türker's text.

the judgment and the "thing" which is the [point of] resemblance of the example [to the other "matter"].[57]

286 || But how can the "example" be dispensable for [showing] the truth of a judgment about a "matter" in which a
2   resemblance [to the example] obtains? This can be | in either of the two ways we discussed in [the section on] "transfer from the evidence to the absent"; namely either
3 | by a [syllogism of] composition in the third figure,[58] or by a [syllogism of] composition in the first figure.[59] It is likely
4   that Aristotle | maintained that the dispensability takes place by a [syllogism of] composition in the first figure.
5   Many [inferences by] "transfer" from an example | to something resembling it take place by mediation of a similarity which is not stated [explicitly], but only the example and that to which the transfer is made are stated
6   [explicitly]. | In many other cases all three [of these components] are stated explicitly.

[57] The initial "judgment" is "This A is T", in the notation of footnote 53 above. The "other matter", B, is thus the connecting link between this judgment on the one hand, and the resemblance-"thing" T on the other, in that "This B is T" is the crucial premiss of the argument.
[58] See above, 274: 5 and following.
[59] See above, 274: 17 and following.

Section 10

CONCLUSION

| With regard to induction and whatever has been enumerated after it,¹ according to what Aristotle said [on the matter], it | is not necessary to attain altogether perfect exactness about the universal which is the basis [of the reasoning]. | Rather, it is sufficient [to achieve exactness] in each one of them in proportion with the measure of knowledge which it provides.² | Because the [syllogistic] "arts"³ in which these statements are used [as premises for reasoning] deal with matters which require a great deal of laxity | in order to be useful in providing knowledge. For if we were perfectly exact in these matters, | then this would exceed the measure of their capacity for it [viz., exactness], and so their usefulness would be overthrown.

| Thus it has been shown that the most demonstrative principle in these [syllogistic] "arts" is the universal principle, | and that the other principles are only able to be fruitful for [reaching] a sought-for conclusion and useful for | [arriving at] a judgment which is not a previously known judgment, when they are carried back to⁴ the universal principle, or | when their force is the force of the universal.⁵

| Thus it has become evident how the statements which

---

¹ That is to say all the materials of sections 7–9 of this treatise, which deal with applications of the syllogism rather than pure theory.

² See above, 282: 12 and following.

³ Cf. 283: 6 and following, above.

⁴ Or: *reduced to.*

⁵ This is obviously the main point which al-Fārābī wishes to leave in the reader's mind with all due emphasis. All really useful and respectable reasoning, no matter how far removed from being syllogistic in character, is to be carried back to, and will derive whatever demonstrative force it possesses from syllogistic inference.

Aristotle called "'convincing' syllogisms"[6] are carried back | to the syllogisms of the assertoric[7] figures. This accomplishes the objective which constitutes our intention here.

| So let this place be the end of this book of ours, God, the All-powerful and the All-high, willing.

| The book is completed. May great thanks be to God. May the blessings of God be upon our master Muḥammad and his righteous kindred.

---

[6] Cf. 275: 17 above.

[7] The assertoric (*jazmiyyah*) figures include both the categorical (*ḥamliyyah*) and the conditional (*sharṭiyyah*).

www.ingramcontent.com/pod-product-compliance
Lightning Source LLC
Chambersburg PA
CBHW031254290426
44109CB00012B/577